EDUCATIONAL STATUS AND EMPOWERMENT OF MUSLIMS

By

Dr. S. Nazeerdeen

Associate Professor
Deptt. of History
Khadir Mohideen College
Adirampattinam
Tanjore Dt.
Tamil Nadu
(India)

DISCOVERY PUBLISHING HOUSE PVT. LTD.
NEW DELHI-110 002

Published by:
Tilak Wasan
DISCOVERY PUBLISHING HOUSE PVT. LTD.
4383/4B, Ansari Road, Darya Ganj
New Delhi-110 002 (India)
Phone : +91-11-23279245, 43596064-65
Fax : +91-11-23253475
E-mail : parul.wasan@gmail.com
discoverypublishinghouse@gmail.com
web : www.discoverypublishinggroup.com

***First Edition:* 2012**

ISBN: 978-93-5056-077-8

Educational Status and Empowerment of Muslims

Printed at:
Shree Balaji Art Press
Delhi

Preface

Education is the panacea for all sorts of social evils. It paves the way for the economic development of a community also. A society can be claimed as more civilized than the others by its educational development only. Such an education had remained a handicap among the Muslim community for a long time. Somehow or the other the Muslim community understood the inevitability of the modern education and began to learn it and followed a better late than never policy. This book deals vividly with the social and educational conditions of the Muslim population of Tamil Nadu. It describes thoroughly the conditions prevailed before as well as after the independence. It traces out the causes for the educational backwardness of the Muslim society and suggests the remedies for them. It throws much light on the various efforts taken by the British government and the Muslim response, the philanthropic munificence and the contribution made by the Tamil Nadu Muslims for the development of modern education. The book focuses on the socio-economic changes brought by the introduction of the modern education among the Muslims. It also describes the status of the Muslim women folk in Tamil Nadu before and after the acceptance of modern education and their empowerment achieved due to it. The author points out the defects of the Muslim society and stresses on the possible efforts that can be taken by the elite of the society to rectify them. He suggests the measures to be taken by the modern Government to improve the educational status of the Muslim community. He also makes an appeal to the affluent Muslims to contribute benevolently for the cause of the education and the Muslim community to pay response and co-operate for the initiatives and efforts taken for their Modern educational development.

Author

Acknowledgements

At the outset, I sincerely record my thanks to my Research Supervisor *Dr. C. K. Sivaprakasam*, M.A., Ph.D., Reader and Head, Post Graduate Department of History, A.V.V.M. Sri Pushpam College (Autonomous), Poondi for his valuable suggestions and efficient guidance.

I express my thanks to the Secretary and Correspondent and the Principal of A.V.V.M. Sri Pushpam College (Autonomous), Poondi for providing me an opportunity to pursue my Ph.D., work as a part time research scholar.

I am thankful to my College Secretary and Correspondent and the Principal for their kind permission and cooperation in carrying out this research work.

I place on record my heartfelt thanks to Dr. K. Rajamanickam, Reader in English, Rajah Serfoji Government Arts College, Thanjavur for his kind help and valuable suggestions in carrying out this research work.

I offer my thanks to Dr. N. Rajendran, Head, Centre for History, Bharathidasan University and the Member of Doctoral Committee for his valuable suggestions and help during the period of my research.

I express my thanks to the members of staff of the Department of History, A.V.V.M. Sri Pushpam College, Poondi and Khadir Mohideen College, Adirampattinam for their cooperation and help in my research.

My thanks are also due to my daughter R.A.Mahjabeen, M.A, M.Phil, D.C.A, who painstakingly read the manuscript and computerized it and helped me in securing the secondary sources.

I offer my profound thanks to the authorities of Tamil Nadu Archives, Chennai; Bharathidasan University Library, Tiruchirappalli; Madras University Library, Chennai; Kannimara Library, Chennai; Saraswathi Mahal Library, Thanjavur; District Collectorate Offices of Tiruchirappalli and Thanjavur; National Archives of India, New Delhi, who supplied me books and source materials.

I also offer my sincere thanks to the authorities of Educational institutions mentioned in this thesis, to all the Respondents to the Questionnaire and to those who gave interviews.

I am also thankful to Mr. Babu Husain Sherriff, for Computer typing the thesis, Xeroxing, Screen-printing and Binding works.

I dedicate this book to my eldest brother J.S.R. Basha, my mentor, whose vision, words and deeds were chiefly responsible for doing this research and my present status.

S. NAZEERDEEN

Contents

List of Abbreviation

A I M A N	-	Abudhabi Indian Muslim Association
B H E L	-	Bharath Heavy Electronics Limited
B T	-	Bachelor of Teaching
G.O	-	Government Order
I M A N	-	Indian Muslim Association
L T	-	Licentiate for Teaching
M E A S I	-	Muslim Educational Association of South India
M I E T	-	Muhammadan Institute of Engineering and Technology
M K N	-	Mohammed Salih, Khadir Mohideen, Naina Muhammed
N A	-	National Archives
OMEIAT	-	Organisation of Muslim Educational Institutions and Association in Tamil Nadu
Pbuh	-	Peace be upon him
S I E T	-	Southern India Educational Trust
S P G	-	Society for Propagation of Gospel
S S L C	-	Secondary School Leaving Certificate
T N A	-	Tamil Nadu Archives
T N T J	-	Tamil Nadu Thouhit Jamath
T M M K	-	Tamil Nadu Muslim Munnetra Kazhagam
U G C	-	University Grants Commission
V M E S	-	Vaniyambadi Muslim Education Society

1

CHAPTER

Introduction

The Holy Quran enjoins education as a duty of every individual and the human knowledge is derived from two principal sources, *'reason'* and *'faith'*. Education is considered as a mark of advancement of human civilization. It distinguishes a cultured society from a barbaric one. Education is significant, fundamental, indispensable and civilized transmission of cultural and non-cultural things. Encyclopaedia Britannica states, *"Education can be thought as the transmission of values and accumulated knowledge of a society."* Bacon says, *"Education is a means to an end."* It develops personality and nationality of individuals. Education can be divided into three phases: Education of an individual, Education of a society and Education of a nation. Education is a continuous process indispensable for the proficient and balanced development of an individual or society. It is a combination of proficient knowledge of Arts, Science, values, customs and traditions, an attainment transmitted to succeeding generations.

The word education is derived from the Latin word *'educare'*, which means 'to bring up'. Hence, it is to develop the noble and intellectual qualities in the minds of the people and make them learn to think with reason. Being the panacea for all kinds of social evils, it plays a decisive role in the socio-economic and political development of a community. Indeed the development of a community is related to the level of attainment it reaches in the field of education. In general, the cultural failure that occurred at the end of the Middle ages in the oriental civilization brought a stagnation in its advancement of arts and science whereas the occidental civilization after the Renaissance advanced very quickly in arts and science and it still continues to be progressing. In India, the Muslims were remotely secluded from the rest of the Muslim world and could not keep link with their counterparts outside India both in material as well as in intellectual advancement. Consequently, their attainments in education were not as high as it was expected. Islam is a rational religion, however wrong interpretations, beliefs and practices crept into the Muslim community. To remove these unwanted elements from the Muslim society religious education alone is not enough. The knowledge of modern education is very helpful to an Aalim (a scholar in Islam) for performing his religious duties in a proper way.

The Muslims for a long time had their own system of education and with that system they were able to produce good citizens, scientists, intellectuals and administrators. But, this education failed to cope with the advancement made in the Western world. When the British introduced the modern western education in India, the Muslims were reluctant to accept it and the majority of the Muslim population kept aloof from it. The present theme is chosen with an aim to bring out the causes for such unwillingness, aloofness and negligence, how they have come up from that syndrome? What made them to accept and take up the modern Western education and how far they have advanced and what are their empowerments in the socio-economic and political fields through that education. The thesis also aims at bringing out the nature of the Muslim Madrasa education (religious), which was followed by the Muslims through centuries and remained as a source of knowledge and wisdom. At the same time, it also aims at highlighting the inadequacy of the Madrasa education in the modern sense and terms.

The hypothesis of the thesis lies in testing the proposition that in the case of non-acceptance of the modern Western education the Muslims would have lagged some hundred years behind in their educational, socio-economic and political spheres of life. It is also presumed that the very acceptance of the Western education, rather the positive response on the part of the Muslims might have been the cause for the awakening of the Muslims and their betterment at the dawn of the twentieth century. The temporary conclusions based on the testing of the hypothesis are formed to have a better understanding on the Muslims' educational condition. For example, if the Muslims had been provided with proper education right from the nineteenth century onwards, they would have become a better community in all avenues.

Review of Literature

The historical and sociological research study on Muslim education in India is scanty. Such research studies were conducted in relation to North India or Central India that too confining to some urban areas. The South India, especially Tamil Nadu, was always neglected by the researchers. A review on the previous works done in this field has left a scope for further studies. Among the several research works done in this field the following are worth mentioning here. *'Education in Madras Presidency'* by Sargurudas and *'History of Education in the Madras Presidency'* by S. Sathiyanathan are two works that describe the educational development in the Madras Presidency in general. *'Madrasa Education in India – A Study of its Past and Present'* (published-1990) by Kuldip Kaur purely deals with Muslims' Madrasa education in India. *'The Political Evolution of Muslims in Tamil Nadu and Madras'*-A.D. 1930-1947 (published-1997) by J.B.P. More focuses on the political development of the Muslims. The research work, *'Education and social changes in South India: Andhra'*-A.D. 1880-1920 (published) by Y. Vaikuntham traces the Social Changes effected by modern education in Andhra Pradesh. *'Muslim Education in Tamil Nadu'*-A.D. 1850-1900 (1994) by S.Abdul

Razack describes the development before A.D. 1900 only. *'History of progress of Education in Madras City'*–A.D. 1854-1947 (1998) by Peer Muhammed mentions the development with regard to Madras city alone. *'Education of Muslim Women in the Presidency of Madras'* with a special reference to the city of Madras–A.D. 1854-1947 (2001) by Hassina Begum portrays mainly on women's education. The above works focus mainly on the general aspects and developments except the work of Dr. Y. Vaikuntham, which traces also the social changes brought in by educational progress. However, there is a desideratum in respect of the theme chosen for this thesis.

This thesis tries to throw light on the Muslims' achievement and their empowerment in the field of education as well as the consequent impact on the political, social and economic activities. The steady progress of education of the Muslims in Tamil Nadu with its origin, growth, relevance, impact and place in changing socio-economic and political systems, has been more than an exercise of academic inquiry and quest of what had really happened.

Scope

Taking cognizance of wide scope of the theme the researcher has chosen to concentrate on those aspects of the theme which have a bearing on the overall growth and development of the education of the Muslims in British India and after that as far as Tamil Nadu is concerned. The scope envisages the study of the British efforts and the Muslim response, the Muslim efforts and the Government response and how could they brought the attention of the Government on their grievances. The study also includes the educational development made by the Muslim community in the post-Independent India. Necessarily the study includes the aspects of the philanthropic efforts of the Muslims, which brought a big break-through in the educational development of the Muslims.

The study demands a focus on the demographic aspects of the Muslim population in Tamil Nadu (broadly divided into Urdu speaking and Tamil speaking) and the contribution made and efforts taken by both sects in general without making a difference. As a sequel the thesis focuses a special reference to the development made in Tiruchirappalli and Thanjavur districts because next to North Arcot the Muslims are more in number and next to Vaniyambadi, early philanthropic efforts have been initiated in these districts.

The present research is confined to Tamil Nadu with a special reference to Tiruchirappalli and Thanjavur districts. The study covers a period from 1882, which marked the formation of Indian Education Commission, to 1967, which marks the end of the Congress Party rule in the Madras State.

Sources

The archival sources form the mainstay of our knowledge for the chosen research. The chief and major source material and information relevant to the theme of thesis found in Madras archives only have been tapped. The report of the Director of Public Instruction, the Administrative Reports of the Madras Presidency, the Educational Index, the Ecclesiastical Reports, the Education Commission Report, the Madras District Manuals, the District Collectorate Reports, the District Gazetteers, the Government Orders (G.Os) and the Native Newspapers,' fortnightly Reports are some of the important sources referred. These sources provide a useful statistical data, which forms an idea for the study of the progress of the education of the Muslims in study area. These records when diligently used in relation to the historical content one had to provide a lot for the development of the thesis. Besides the above, many primary records collected from the various sources, viz. The Muslim philanthropists, elites of the society, religiously well learned persons were consulted. In addition to that many souvenirs, newspapers, journals and magazines were also referred to. The above sources when diligently consulted reveal many aspects of the theme. For the period after Independence, the interview and questionnaire method has been a useful exercise.

Scheme

The thesis is planned to bring out the salient features of the development of education of the Muslims and their empowerment between the last quarter of the nineteenth century and the middle of the twentieth century in seven chapters including Introduction and Conclusion. The demography of the Muslims of the Madras State, curriculum of the Hindu elementary and higher education, the Muslim concept of education, the Muslim Maktab and Madrasa education and a survey of important Madrasas working in Tamil Nadu have been described in the First Chapter i.e. Introduction itself as a necessary backdrop for the study. The Second Chapter deals with the attitude of the Muslims towards education at the close of the nineteenth century. The Chapter next describes the British efforts and the Muslim response between 1901 and 1947. The Fourth Chapter gives an account of the Muslim efforts before and after Independence. The Fifth Chapter deals exclusively with the Muslim philanthropic munificence in Thanjavur and Tiruchirappalli districts with their historical background. The Chapter Sixth mainly focuses the socio-economic changes and the empowerment of Muslims, which includes female education also. The Chapter on Conclusion summarises the findings in the preceding chapters and gives various suggestions and steps needed to be taken for the development of the education of the Muslims. The thesis deals with a special reference to the education of the Muslims of Tiruchirappalli and Thanjavur districts. So, a brief history of the two districts has been mentioned here.

HISTORICAL BACKDROP

Topography and Demography

The Madras Presidency was the southern most province of the then British Indian Empire. The total area of the Madras Presidency was 1,41,705 square miles. And it was about 20,000 square miles larger than that of the United Kingdom.[1] By about 1901 the Madras Presidency comprised 22 districts, the people of these districts belonged to five major linguistic areas

Map 1.1 : The Madras Presidency during the British Period

of Tamil, Telugu, Malayalam, Kanarese, Oriya and others.[2] Later, the Tamil districts were separated from the Madras Presidency and formed into the Madras State which was renamed as Tamil Nadu in 1968. The present Tamil Nadu has an area of 1,30,058 square kilometre and comprising 30 districts. As according to 2001 census the population of Tamil Nadu is 6,24,05,679. Among this, 5,49,85,079 of them are Hindus, 34,70,647 of them are Muslims and 37,85,060 of them are Christians.[3]

Tiruchirappalli is the central most district in the Madras state. The river Cauvery transverses the central portion of the district making it a fertile basin. Tiruchirappalli is a famous city in South India and is located on the southern bank of the Cauvery. The well-known Srirangam temple is located on the island formed by the Cauvery and its distributary Coleroon. Tiruchirappalli is an important educational centre in the state. The economy of the district is essentially agrarian in character. It has also a few household industries. Of late, an attempt has been made to develop the district industrially. In the agricultural field, the development has been good, but economic prosperity has varied from tract to tract. Only limited deposits of minerals are found. In the absence of any local initiative, the possibility of any pronounced industrial development is necessarily limited. But it has not witnessed any technological development, which can provide an adequate basis for rapid Industrialization. The people have taken to Western Education and have been more interested in service-oriented tasks. The district has great cultural and historical importance, but has not achieved any significant role in the economy of the state before the establishment of big industries like BHEL.

After the establishment of British supremacy in India, many places were brought under the British East India Company's rule. Tiruchirappalli also came under the British administration and an English Collector was appointed in 1801. Soon after the area was ceded to the British East India Company and many administrative changes took place.

Tiruchirappalli was annexed with Thanjavur district and then once again made as a separate district.[4]

In the Tiruchirappalli district, we could see various castes and communities living together harmoniously. The major communities found in the district are caste Hindus, Schedule caste divisions, Muslims and Christians. The Brahmins in the district are found predominantly in the Cauvery delta region. The Christian population in the district is larger than that of other districts because of intensive Missionary activities. Among the Muslim population the Urdu speaking people are mostly officials and the Tamil-speaking Muslim people are mostly business oriented.[5]

The Hindus accounted for 92.73 per cent of the total population during 1911. Their percentage in district population had shown a slow but definite trend to decline and it had touched the mark of 90.28 per cent in 1961. As a contrast to this trend noticed among the Hindus, the Christians and the Muslims had shown a sure tendency to increase. The percentage of Christians in total population was only 4.15 per cent in 1911, but it had risen to 5.38 per cent in 1961. Similarly the percentage of Muslims had also recorded an increase from 3.12 per cent in 1911 to 4.03 per cent in 1961.[6]

Thanjavur district is known as the granary of Tamil Nadu. It has a glorious history behind it. It was the seat of Chola power when Tamil Nadu reached its zenith of glory. It has a rich and varied cultural heritage. It is one of the coastal districts; its coastline extending over 140 miles turns southwest at point Calimere. The sea board can be divided into two sections, one extending almost 72 miles from the mouth of the river Coleroon to point Calimere in the south and the other bordering the Palk Strait for about 68 miles from point Calimere. The district can be described as a vast fertile soil with a gentle but definite slope towards the sea. The region can be divided into three distinct divisions, viz., the deltaic region, the upland area and the salt swamp.

Thanjavur's economy is essentially agrarian, its agriculture being sustained by a network of irrigation sources and improved method of cultivation. Thanjavur had the highest degree of education in the whole Presidency, among the male population only 37.81 percent of those of 15 years of age and upwards were illiterate.[7] Literacy rate of Thanjavur district was high because of Brahmin and Muslim population.

The following statement will give an idea about the social composition of the district, as the demography is more or less similar to that of Tiruchirappalli except with some changes in its coastal areas. Kallars are the majority people among the caste Hindus living all over the district, concentrated more around Thanjavur and Mannargudi taluks. Vanniyars are found majority in Kumbakonam and Mayavaram taluks. Schedule caste people are living all over the district concentrated more in Thiruthuraipoondi taluk. Muthiraiyar and Ambalakarar or Vellalar communities are found more around Pattukkottai and Aranthangi taluks. Even though the Brahmins are a minority distributed all around the district, they are found more in number at Kumbakonam and Mayavaram. The Muslim population in the district is found more in the coastal areas such as Nagapattinam, Nagoor, Muthupet, Koothanallur and Adirampattinam.[8] The Muslims found in the coastal areas like Adirampattinam are called as Maraikkayars and the other Muslims are called as Rawthers.

The total population of the district has increased from 2,982,670 in 1951 to 3,245,927 during 1961 thus recording an 8.83 per cent increase during the decade. The Hindus have recorded only a low percentage in increase viz., 7.98. Muslims along with the Hindus have recorded only a lower percentage increase than the increase recorded by the district population. The increase in their number was of the order of 7.6 per cent only. As a contrast to these, the Christians have recorded 23.24 per cent rise during the same period.[9]

The 1961 Census has recorded 37.38 percent rise in the district population over the 1911 position. During the same period running over five decades, various religious groups have recorded 35.86 per cent increase over 1911, while Muslims have recorded 55.40 per cent rise and the Christians 35.24 per

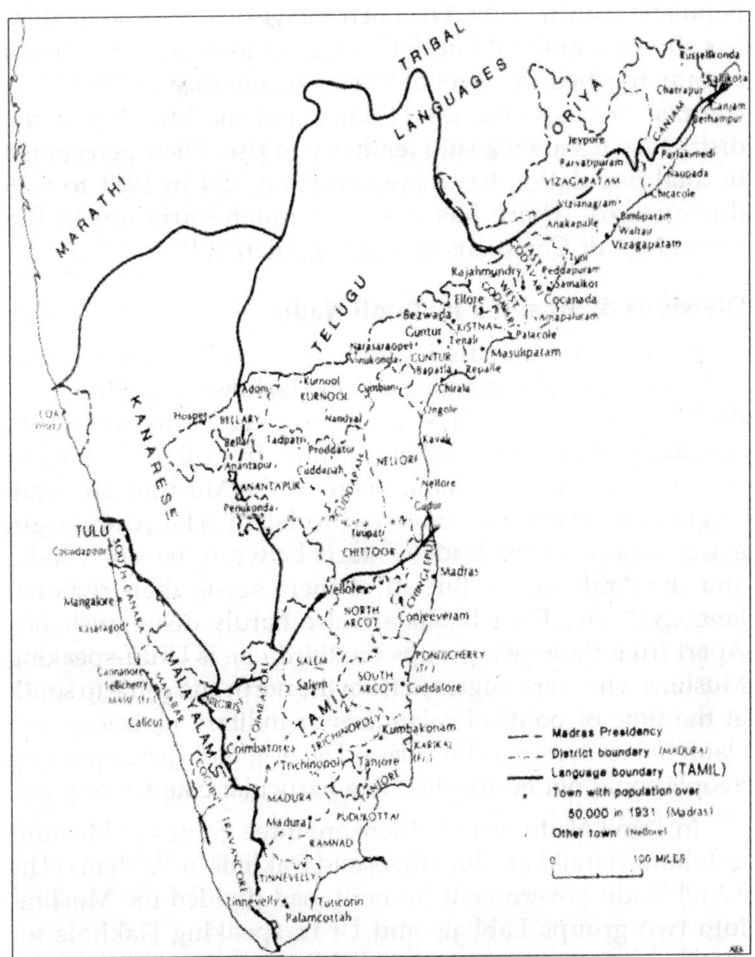

Map 1.2 : Districts in Madras Presidency—Before Independence

cent. As is clear from these figures, the Muslims have recorded the highest increase over the last few decades.[10]

The Hindus accounted for 90.62 per cent of the total population during 1911. Their percentage in district population has shown a gradual but definite trend to decline and it has already touched the level of 89.60 per cent during 1961. As a contrast to this trend, the Hindus, and the Muslims of the district have shown a sure tendency to rise. Their percentage to total population has increased from 5.54 in 1911 to 6.26 during 1961. There has not been much variation in the percentage of Christians to total population.[11]

Divisions of Muslims in Tamil Nadu

Islam has no caste distinction. However a sort of class divisions is prevailing among Indian Muslims especially among the Muslims of the Madras Presidency. The Muslims of South are maintaining their identity distinct from the Muslims of North India. In South India many of the Muslims are Arab origin and others are converted to Islam. The Arab origin exists because of the trade contacts between the south India and the Arab world. But all of them speak their regional language only. Their habits are also hardly distinguishable. Apart from these two groups the third one is Urdu-speaking Muslims who were migrated from the north and came to south at the time of political calamities or military invasions and claim themselves as ruling class. The origin of Urdu speaking people could not be attached to a particular country or place.

In Tamil Nadu, mainly there are three groups of Muslims as follow Maraikkars, Rawthers and Dakhnis or Patthans (The Tamil Nadu government formerly had divided the Muslims into two groups Labbais and Urdu speaking Dakhnis for offering scholarships. Later all Muslims are categorically considered as backward class).

Maraikkayars

They are traditionally traders. Once they had commercial contact with Ceylon, Malaysia and Arabia. Because of their trade they are rich and influential. The Maraikkayars are found only along the sea coast of Tamil Nadu, Pondicherry, Karaikal, Nagapattinam, Adirampattinam, Keelakarai, Kayalpattinam etc. The Maraikkayars are also known as Labbais because of their learned distinction. Among them there were Tamil scholars and poets and their contribution to Tamil literature is highly appreciable. They follow 'Shafi' school of thought of Islam.

Rawthers

The second group of Muslims is Rawthers. They are inland Muslims living all over Tamil Nadu. They are converted to Islam from the various castes found in Tamil Nadu. The word Rawther was originally used to point out to one who trained the horses. Once this word Rawther was used to denote horseman irrespective of their religion like 'Mahutan' (elephant tamer) but in due course of time it came to be known as a class of Muslims. There are slight cultural differences prevailing between the Maraikkayars and the Rawthers. The Rawthers mostly follow Hanafi school of thought of Islam. There are Labbais (used as an attitude to denote learned quality) in Maraikkayars as well as in Rawthers.

Dakhnis or Deccanis (The Urdu Speaking Muslims)

The third groups of Muslims are those who speak Urdu or have Urdu language as their mother tongue. They are known as Dakhni Muslims i.e. Deccani Muslims. They are also called as 'Patthans'. Long ago they migrated to Tamil Nadu from north India at the time of political calamities and invasions. Their language, culture, dress, customs and manners are different from other Muslims. They consider themselves as ruling class owing to their military origin. Their population is more at Madras, Madurai, Trichy, North Arcot, South Arcot etc. They are mostly followers of the Hanafi school of thought in Islam and they marry among themselves.

Even though these differences are prevailing among the Muslims there is no casteism. They live in equal terms and now-a-days they even perform marriage alliances with one another. All the Muslim rulers of India (Delhi sultans and Mughals) belonged to Hanafi School of thought. The travellers and soldiers who came to India through the Khyber and Polan passes were all Hanafis. The Arab Muslim traders who came to India by sea belong to Shafi School of thought. So, we could see most of the offshore region Muslims, especially the Maraikkayars of Adirampattinam, belong to Shafi sect of school of thought.

The Muslims are mostly mercantile people and landowners. The Maraikkayars' predominant characteristic feature in the past was trading with foreign countries like Sri Lanka and South East Asia. Because of the change of the trend and scenario in those countries their mercantile activities suffered and almost stopped. At present the Muslims in the Thanjavur district particularly from the coastal areas are seeking their fortunes in the Gulf and the Western countries as skilled and unskilled workers in all types of jobs. The Brahmins in this district are mostly high officials and priests in the temples.[12] The Muslims of Tanjore are most numerous in the inland taluks like Kumbakonam and Papanasam, but they also abound in the trading coastal taluks of Nagapattinam and Pattukkottai, (Adirampattinam). They are mostly Labbais and Maraikkayars; Urdu speaking Dakhni Muslims are the negligible minority.

The word Labbai seems to be of recent (Sonogars) origin, for merely the Labbais were called Sonogars, meaning natives of Sonogam (Arabic). They are in fact, partly the descendants of the Arab traders of refugees who married women of this coast and partly the descendants of Hindus who converted to Islam. The name Maraikkayars is derived from the Arabic 'Markaba' means 'the boat'. They are also like the Lebbais, a mixed race of the Arabs and the Hindus and are mostly traders. They, however, belong to the Shafi sect. They admit converts from various Hindu classes (called Tulukkais) but they generally do not intermarry with them.[13] The Maraikkayars consider themselves superior to the Labbais and do not generally inter drive or inter marry with them. The Muslims of pure descent, on the other hand, hold both the Maraikkayars and the Labbais inferior to them and do not inter marry with them (these practices have gone out now due to the spread of Modern education). This has led to the Maraikkayars and the Labbais adopting some of the customs of the pure Muslims like dressing themselves and their women in strict Muslim fashion and by speaking Hindustani at Home.[14]

Education before the Advent of British

Before the advent of the British to India, there were four ancient methods of Education. They were, the instruction given by the Brahmins to their disciples, the seats of Sanscrit learning, the Maktabs and Madrasas or the Schools and Colleges of Mohammedans and a large number of Village schools. The latter gave an elementary education to the trading classes, to the children of petty landholders and well to do families among the cultivators; but they did not share in the endowments of the Government.[15]

The Maktabs are the primary stage of Muslim education and mostly attached with mosques. In Maktabs the children were taught the Arabi alphabets, rudimentary knowledge of religion and reciting the Quran without knowing the meaning. The Madrasas are the institutions of higher learning of the Muslim education. In Madrasas everything about Islam is taught and the persons who finished their education from these institutions are called as Aalims (religious scholar).

The indigenous education found in the Madras Presidency was universal as in other parts of India, long before the commencement of the British rule in India. In every Hindu matt or monastery and in every large Town or Village with Brahmin residents, instruction in some branches of Sanskrit learning, or in the Tamil classics and Pooranas had been taught from time immemorial. This was the recognized feature of the every village school. The Villages, large or small had from a very early date had its own school.[16] The description of such education at the present day is equivalent to the description of what it was a century or two back, for no change perceptible.

The Muslim Concept of Education

The Arabic word 'Ilm' is used to refer to knowledge, which ultimately refers to education. The foundation of the Muslim education stands mainly on two pillars—Quran and Sunnah. It is therefore natural that educational schemes of Muslims are inclined towards religion. The main aim of education is 'To understand the relation of Man with God, as revealed in the Holy Quran.' All educational activities of the Muslims in Madrasas have been and continue to be governed by this aim, though there might have been different approaches. In fact, the religious aim of Islamic education is the service to God and it is the highest object of teaching and studying the preparation of all mortals for the other world, with purity of Niyyat (aim). Islam has not only permitted the study of Science useful for civic and social purposes, but has, at times, even made it obligatory. Its study has never been interdicted on religious grounds. In fact Islam does not permit the use of religious means to attain secular ends. It also stresses that if a man acquires intellectualism with no 'faith' it does not serve any purpose in front of God, instead if he has faith as his basic thing on which he constructs his intellectualism he becomes an embodiment of virtue and epitome of success.

Introduction of English Education and the Muslim Indifference

When the British rule was established in India, the East India Company continued to follow the Persian language as the official language, which was in practice at the time of the Muslim rulers. The expansion of the territory and more involvement in administrative matters compelled the British to introduce the English language among the masses. It is an obvious truth that the need for a large body of employees for clerical work, the English education was introduced. But it was not systematically introduced. In the beginning the Schools were started by the missionaries, supported by the British East India Company. The Muslims saw these Christian missionary schools with a suspicious eye that their institutions were nothing but centers of conversion, which was also a truth to some extent. The Christian missionaries took education and medicine as a two way process to spread their religion in India. But such motives and missionary activities were not found among the Muslims. This was the main handicap present with the Muslims in the promotion of education. The Christian missionaries also did not take keen interest on the promotion of the education among the Muslims, because they understood that teaching Christianity to the Muslims was more difficult than to the Hindus.

The change over from Persian to English as the official language did not affect the Muslims of Madras Presidency, because Urdu and Tamil are the wide spoken languages of the Muslims of this region. So, the reluctant attitude of Muslims towards English education was not pertaining to the language problem, the problem was the sovereignty of the British over the Muslims. The main cultural differences between Muslims and British people were another cause for the aversion of Western education by the Muslims. The Church in India allowed the people who converted to Christianity to have their old names with that of the Christian names and also permitted them to follow their old culture and way of life. This sort of flexibility was not allowed in Islam and the Muslims considered that their faith must be followed without any changes introduced by the human efforts. The British Government introduced English education, which was heartily welcomed by the leading Hindus but the feelings of the Muslims were not quite friendly.

As the British Sanskrit scholar, H.H. Wilson put it: "Upon the proposal to appropriate all the funds to English education there was a petition from the Mohammedans of Calcutta, signed by about 8,000 people, including all the most respectable Maulvis and native gentlemen of the city. After objecting to it upon general principles they said that the evident object of the Government was the conversion of natives; and they encouraged English exclusively and discouraged Mohammedan and Hindu studies, because they wanted to include the people to become Christian."[17] In order to allay these suspicions Lord William Bentinck enunciated a policy of strict religious neutrality: "In all schools and colleges...........interference and injudicious tampering with the religious belief of the students mingling direct or indirect teaching of Christianity with the system of instructions ought to be positively forbidden."[18] This policy of religious neutrality was not accepted by the missionaries who had founded a number of institutions all over the country with their full-fledged activities. The Muslims who were reluctant were not brought under the missionary efforts in promoting their education, which was also a cause for the educational backwardness of the Muslims.

The Muslim contribution to the development of education and learning during the mediaeval period was indeed noteworthy and great considering both in theory and practice. The impact of Islam was also felt in the languages found in India. The Muslims had contributed to the various branches of science, arts and literatures of India. Highlighting these achievements, the study also discusses how the Muslims have failed to keep pace with the fast changing modern world and tries to bring out the extent to which Muslim backwardness could be attributed to demote their educational development in the modern period and it suggests how the existing condition could be fruitfully modified.

The advent of Europeans and the establishment of the British rule in India though opened a new era yet it hampered the Muslim interest politically in particular. The Muslims who claimed to be the ruling class could not tolerate the reversal of their fortune and even went to the level of thinking that the learning of English will spoil their religious faith and culture. "Muslims looked back with pride to the glories which had vanished with hopelessness to the calamities which they further held in store."[19] The introduction of English, which replaced the Persian language, jeopardized the Muslim interest in administration.

When the British offered facilities for western learning the Hindus responded to it especially the Brahmins and availed themselves of the opportunities, whereas, the Muslims hesitated and declined to accept and utilize facilities and patronage offered by the British as the result of this attitude. The Hindus received their share in the administration and got appointments in the various Government departments. Thus, the Hindu community started to rise in knowledge in official position and in wealth. The Muslims considered themselves as, "A race ruined under British rule."[20] They opposed to the new system of public instruction because it was against their traditions and religious beliefs. This attitude or the opinion of the Muslims was superstitious and baseless. Islam does not just pertain to Arabia or to one sect of people alone. Instead, Islam is for all, language, caste, creed and race cannot be a barrier to it. So, the faith of a Muslim could not be collapsed just by learning English or Western Science. The conservative Muslim people of those days failed to understand this truth. "If you want to drive English out of Hindustan learn English", said, Sir Syed Ahmed khan. Because of the backward policy of the conservative Muslims, the community suffered socially, economically, educationally and politically. The crying need of the moment was to try to overcome the reluctance of the Indian Muslims to adapt themselves to their changed circumstances and at the same time to gain the confidence of the British who looked upon Muslims with suspicion and distrust.

Sir William Hunter in his book, 'The Indian Musalmans', published in 1871, pointed out that the entire Muslim community had been disloyal and a source of chronic danger to the British power. And he also pleaded for rallying the Muslims round the British Government by removing their genuine grievances. The work of reconciliation with the British besides social reforms and educational development was not an easy task.

Complexity of a Muslim Student

When the Western education was introduced in India, the Indians particularly Muslims had to pursue different types of education and had to follow different types of Schools. A Muslim boy or girl first went to a Maktab or Madrasa and then to a normal school for secular education, whereas a Hindu boy or girl straight away went to a normal school to get his or her education. This kind of difficulty was with Muslim community only because the Muslims gave importance to their religious education. The above said factor was to be considered as one of the causes for the educational backwardness of the Muslim community. Madrasas are custodians of the values of the Muslim Community and the guardians of its heritage. According to Muslims, they have been able to preserve and safeguard their culture through these institutions, which have made such adjustments and changes as necessary in due course. Now-a-days, this practice is vanishing away from the Muslims. The children under the age of 10 are attending the Maktabs attached to the mosques early morning only. Now, only a section of the Muslim population is taking up the higher religious education in the Madrasas.

REFERENCES

1. *Imperial Gazetteer of India,* Provincial Series, Madras, Vol. I, Usha Publications, New Delhi, 1985, p. 1.
2. *Ibid.*
3. *Census of India-2001,* the First Report on Religion.
4. *District Census Hand Book, Tiruchirappalli, 1901-70,* Chap. I, pp. 2–4, Tamil Nadu Archives (T.N.A.).
5. *Ibid.*
6. *Ibid.,* p. 13.
7. *Census of India, 1891,* p. 179, T.N.A.
8. *District Census Hand Book, Thanjavur, 1901-70,* p. 33, T.N.A.
9. F.R. Hemingway, ICS, *Madras District Gazetteers, Tanjore, 1906,* (Edited by Francis, ICS) Education, p. 162, T.N.A.

10. *Ibid.*, p. 163.
11. *Ibid.*
12. B.S. Baliga, *Thanjavur District Hand Book, 1957*, p. 274, T.N.A.
13. Edgar Thurston, *Caste and Tribes of South India*, Vol. IV, 1909, pp. 198-205, T.N.A.
14. *Gazetteers of Tanjore District*, 1915, Vol. I, pp. 60-61, T.N.A.
15. *Manual of the Administration of the Madras Presidency*, Vol. II, p. 563.
16. *Ibid.*, p. 565.
17. Syed Noorullah and Naik, J.P., *History of Education in India*, Bombay, 1951, p. 92.
18. *Ibid.*
19. Hampton, *S.V., Biographical Studies in Modern Indian Education*, p. 213.
20. Hunter, W.W., *The Indian Musalmans*, 1871, p. 149.

CHAPTER 2

Muslim Attitude Towards Western Education at the Close of the Nineteenth Century

The foundation of the British paramountcy in India marks the beginning of a new epoch in the history of the country. It also marks the introduction of a new educational system in India. When the Western education was introduced in India, the attitude of the Muslim community in the beginning towards it was very hostile. The attitude of the Muslims of the Madras Presidency in the earlier stage towards the Western education, the reasons alleged by them for keeping aloof from the education offered in the Government schools, the gradual changes in their attitude, the measures taken by the British Government to improve the educational condition of the Muslims, the results of the steps taken by the Government, the early efforts of the Muslims in the cause of education, the traditional practices of the Musalman schools, the requests of the Muslims to start schools in their region and by the last quarter of the nineteenth century how the above mentioned factors developed, interacted and reinforced one another in such a way that they effected in the creation of a new type of conditions and values in the educational life of the Muslims have been discussed hereunder.

The British East India Company as a private body never took keen interest in the promotion of Education to the Indians but in due course it felt the need for it. When Warren Hastings founded the Calcutta Madarasa in 1781, he had the main objective on the Muslims, "To qualify the sons of Mohammedan gentlemen for responsible and lucrative offices in the State."[1] But to bring this policy to practice was of a great task to the British East India Company. There was no proper Educational system existed in those times. The educational institutions present at that time did not suit the Modern education. Only very few institutions were available to impart higher education to a hand full of students in the state. The collectors of the various places were asked to give a report on the actual state of education throughout the country to the Governor of the Madras Presidency. The report submitted showed that there were no educational institutions in the modern sense, but there were a few places imparting knowledge in the higher branches of learning to a limited number of students.

Early Efforts in the Cause of Mohammedan Education

In 1781, when Warren Hastings founded the Calcutta Madarasa, it was designed, "To qualify the Mohammedans of Bengal for the public service......and to enable them to compete on more equal terms with the Hindus for employment under Government. Some fifty years later, after the introduction of English (Education) into the course of studies, the council of Education had to confess that the endeavour to impart a high order of English education to the Mohammedan community had completely failed."[2] Forty years later again, "The condition of the Mohammedan population of India, as regard to education had off late been frequently pressed upon the attention of the Government of India."[3] The Mohammedans neither competed on equal terms with the Hindus for employment under the Government, nor had the endeavor to bring success to their community. Matters were, no doubt in a promising condition than in 1832, and as regards the general spread of education, it was a much more promising condition than in 1792. A considerable proportion of Mohammedans were learning English, a large proportion were in schools of one kind or another. But the higher education was not cultivated, in any appreciable degree, more extensively than it had been in 1832.

Causative Factors for Non-chalance of the Mohammedans

The causes, which deterred the Mohammedans from such cultivation, were debated even among themselves. While some held that the absence of instruction in tenets of their faith; and at still more the injurious effects of English education in creating a disbelief in religion, were the main obstacles, others were of the opinion that religion had little to do with the question.

The following causes for their holding aloof from the Western education are attributed:

Some contended the system of education prevailing in Government schools and colleges corrupted the morals and manners of the pupils, and that for this reason the better classes would not subject their sons to dangerous contact. There was only less number of Mohammedan teachers in Government institutions. The unwillingness of Government Educational Officers to accept the counsel and co-operation of Mohammedans and the numerous minor faults in the departmental system, the comparatively small progress in real learning made by the pupils in Government schools, the practice among the well-to-do Mohammedans in educating their children at home, the indolence and improvidence which were too common among them, their hereditary love for the profession of arms and mercantile activities, the absence of friendly intercourse between Mohammedans and Englishmen, the unwillingness felt by the better born to associate with those lower in the social scale. Poverty was nearly general among Mohammedans. The coldness of Government towards the Muslim race after the Sepoy Mutiny of 1857 was antagonistic. The books of the Government schools had a tone, which was hostile, or scornful towards the Mohammedan religion.[4] The Muslims feared that the customs and manners of the British would spoil their culture.

These and a varied other causes had been put forward at different times by Mohammedans for their scanty appreciation for English education. All such causes may have combined towards a general result, but a candid Mohammedan would probably admit that the most powerful factors are to be found in the pride of the race, a memory of the bygone superiority, religious fears, and a not unnatural attachment to the learning of Islam. But whatever the causes, the facts remained; though the enquiries made in 1871-73 went to prove that except in the matter of the higher education there had been a tendency to exaggerate the backwardness of the Mohammedans.[5]

Measures taken in Madras Presidency

Upon the receipt of the resolution of the Government of India, to improve the educational condition of the Muslims, the Government of Madras invited the Syndicate of the University to consider whether any steps could be taken to attract a larger number of Mohammedans for graduation. In its reply the syndicate of Madras University expressed an opinion that, "The regulation of the University should not be modified with the view of encouraging a particular section of the population, but that the Musalmans should be treated in precisely the same manner as all other inhabitants of the Madras Presidency…and while deploring the undoubted fact of the Mohammedans being behind the Hindus as regards educational progress, they did not see that any steps could be taken by the university to modify this state of things."[6] The steps taken by the Director of Public Instruction was not more encouraging. He considered that the department had done all that it could do for Mohammedans education, and pointed out that a special concession had been made to Musalman students by exempting them from few regulations regarding the fees.

The Government of Madras was, however, convinced that the existing scheme of instruction was framed with too exclusive reference to the requirements of Hindu students, and that Mohammedans were placed at, so great disadvantage that the wonder was, not that the Mohammedan element in the schools was so small, but that it existed at all. The Governor in council, therefore, issued orders that the Director should, without delay, "Take steps with a view to the establishment of elementary schools at Arcot and Ellore, and corresponding classes in the existing schools at the principal centers of the Mohammedan population, such as Trichinopoly, Cuddapah, Kurnool, and perhaps Mangalore, in which instructions were given in the Hindustani language, and Mohammedan boys may thus acquire such a knowledge of English language and of the elementary branches of instruction as will qualify them for admission in to the higher classes of the Zillah and provincial schools and other similar instruction..." Arrangements were also, without loss of time, made for the training of Mohammedan teachers, and instruction in Persian was to be provided in any high school in which there was a sufficient number of Mohammedans.[7]

Results of the Measures Taken

The statistics of the year 1880-81 indicates the measures taken during the interval and the results obtained were as follows: The special schools maintained by Government were 11 in number, 7 of them being Anglo-vernacular Middle schools, and 4 Anglo-vernacular Primary schools. Nine schools of Anglo-vernacular or vernacular were maintained by Municipalities, and of aided schools with a special provision for Musalman pupils. There were 4 Anglo-vernacular, and 210 vernacular schools. Other inducements had also been held out to Musalman students. They were admitted in all schools upon payment of half the usual fees, seven scholarships were especially reserved for Musalman candidates at the University examinations; a special Deputy Inspector of Musalman schools had been appointed; an elementary normal school had been established at Madras. They still continued to allot the Arabic and Persian languages at its examinations with a maximum of marks considerably larger than that carried by vernacular languages.[8] The combined results of these measures were eminently satisfactory. In place of the 5,531 Musalmans at school in 1870-71, the returns for 1880-81 give 22,075 or 6.7 per cent of the total number under instruction, while the percentage of Musalmans to the total population of the Presidency is only 6 per cent. The proportion of boys at school to those of a school going age is for Mohammedans 15.1, for Hindus 13.7. But it is not in numbers only that progress has been made. Considering the results of the Middle school examinations, the percentage of passed candidates to those examined was, for Hindus (non-Brahmins) 35, for Mohammedans 41. In the lower University examinations taking only the percentage of successful candidates to those examined the results for 1880-81 are equally satisfactory.[9]

In the entrance Examination, the percentage of Hindus other than Brahmins and of Musalmans is thus practically the same. It must be remembered, however, that the proportion of students to population is about three times as great for Hindus (including Brahmins) as for Musalmans. In the latter case, the percentage of passed candidates is even more favorable to the Musalmans; but the proportion of candidates to population is five times as great as Hindus (including Brahmins) as for Musalmans. Of college education beyond the First examination in Arts, Mohammedans, in general, did not avail themselves at all, though there is no reason to suppose that the general system of education beyond that standard is not as well suited to the Mohammedans as that below it. The attendance of the Musalman students in the various institutions, both Government aided and unaided, as compared with the total attendance, was not fair in 1881-82.[10]

The schools to which the Muslims went varied from one part of the country to another but a common characteristic was that they all imparted knowledge of the Quran, however rudimentary. Many of these schools were assigned yeomiahs and money grants. There were Madrasas where daily food was provided to the pupils.[11] Grants and Inams were given to teachers also. But in most cases the teacher in a Madrasa had to depend entirely on the gifts of the parents and his functions extended even beyond the four walls of the Madrasa.[12]

Generally every mosque of the Muslim community is combined with the elementary school called Maktab. The Muslim children used to go to these Maktabs early in the morning to get basic knowledge of the Quran, that is learning alphabets and the Quran. Other than this nothing more is taught there. To get elementary education the children have to go to other normal schools. The Christian missionaries were running such schools. But, "It must not be supposed that there was little or no education in India before the Christian missionaries took it up. There was more than a little. Every Hindu village had its school, its Pyall or verandah school, every Muslim mosque had its teachers in the elementary schools of the Legal scholarship which has distinguished so many Qazis in past times…what the missionaries did was to give education a new direction."[13] Domestic instruction by the Moulvi arranged by men of substance for their own children, where some children of modest means might also participate was also prevalent on a considerable scale.[14] The Madrasas catered to the educational needs of those who wished to go in for Higher Arabic studies. Here 'Higher Arabic studies' means learning the meaning of the Quran, grammar, Shariah (laws) etc.

When the political control of India had gradually transferred from the Natives to the East India Company and the British exercised their authority and administration over the Hindus and Muslims of India, the Hindus took it as a usual transformation, whereas the Muslims looked it with great resentment and looked back with pride to the glories which had vanished.[15] One of the results of the British administration was the slow but steady spread of English education and the substitution of English for Persian as the language of administration and official business. The Muslims viewed with dismay the redisplacement of Persian and they held themselves aloof from a policy, which had dealt a heavy blow to their culture and was even calculated to undermine their faith. As pointed out by the Education Commission of 1882, the untoward actions of the Government officials against the Mohammedans pushed them to follow non-cooperation with Government proposals. The affluent people of Muslim community failed to understand their social responsibility of eradicating mass illiteracy of their people. This condition was further worsened by the inimical attitude against each other (i.e. Muslims and the British people). However large scale educational work was organized in the country by the Education Department of the Government unmindful of the Muslim response. The Government was expecting a change of mind from the Muslims.[16]

The Hindus availed themselves of the facilities offered for the acquisition of western knowledge and got appointments, whereas the Muslims had a disproportionate share in the administration and judicial appointments. The Christians were making headway in education and public service, thanks to the devotion and generosity of the Christian missionaries of various denominations. A missionary like Caldwell could not be amazed at the indifference of the Muslims to formal education in secular schools.[17] In consequence, "The relative position of the Hindu and Mohammedan communities steadily changed, the former rising in knowledge, wealth and influence and the latter declining."[18] This unnatural reversal of fortune not only made the Muslims sullen and despondent but they also started to regard themselves as "a race ruined under British rule."[19] They complained that the new system of Public Instruction was, "Opposed to the traditions, unsuited to the requirements and hateful to the religion of the Musalmans."[20] Generally majority of the Muslims had dislike towards the English language and western education but few came forward to study the western education and English language as a challenge in response. On seeing the interest shown by the minority of the Muslim community the British East India Company also took steps.

Sir Thomas Munro, the Governor of Madras took interest in local people's education and made an enquiry regarding its status. He not only surveyed the various districts but also drew up a scheme for the maintenance of schools at every district and set up a committee of Public Instruction for carrying out the scheme. He did yeoman service to the educational system of the Madras Presidency.[21] The committee, afterwards amalgamated with the College Board and became the Board of Public Instruction in 1826.Thomas Munro broadly indicated his views in that minute as follows: "We ought to extend to our Mohammedans the same advantages of education as to our Hindu subjects and perhaps even in a greater degree because a greater portion of them belong to the middle and higher classes. But as their number is not more than one twentieth of that of the Hindus it will not be necessary to give more than one Mohammedan school to each Collectorate, except in Arcot and a few other Collectorates where the Mohammedan population is considerably above the usual standard."[22] Forty teachers were recruited from each district one Hindu and one Muslim were to be selected.

Early Requests of the Muslims to Start Schools

There were many requests from Muslims of different parts of Madras Presidency to start schools in their locality. For instance, in 1829 the Governor sanctioned a Thasildary school at Tiruchirappalli at the request of the local Muslims and appointed one Sayed Wali Sahib, recommended by them as teacher.[23] The Muslims of Kumbakonam succeeded in getting sanction for a school for themselves.[24] The Muslims of Nagore made a similar representation to the Principal Collector of Tanjore in 1830 and orders were issued for a school to be provided for them.[25] In 1835 a Thasildary school was opened at Vellore at the request of the Muslims there.[26]

The proposals of starting schools in various places were discussed in the Court of Directors and the recommendations made by the Government were approved by it. The proposal materialized and the school was started only in 1851. The time seemed to be most opportune. There was a change in the attitude of a section of the Muslims towards western education. Balfour, the Government agent at Chepauk, who was close to the Muslims in Madras and knew them more intimately than any one else, remarked, "A slight change has occurred among the Mohammedan community of Triplicane and Mylapore, there being now observable amongst them a desire for instruction and knowledge, that was better than the apathetic ignorance which they were contented with before, the more so because the desire above noticed is still increasing and is likely now from the causes in operation, permanently to continue." He advised secular education and also insisted that the school should be opened to all Muslims. The Nawab agreed to it. In fact the Nawab also had in mind a secular education that would help the Muslims to secure employment in Government services. His letter to Balfour said that, he was starting the school "Because it would be a means of encouragement to the students to educate themselves and be fully qualified and competent for getting their livelihood by being employed in public offices, after obtaining certificate of proficiency at a Final Public examination which will, in communication with the Government be conducted by such persons as will be selected by Government."[27] During the period of British East India company a most fruitful private attempt to establish a school was made by the then Carnatic Nawab Wallajah in 1851.This school, named Madhrasa-I-Azam after Nawab Azamjah, went through many vicissitudes, but still flourished as a Government institution.[28]

Normally in elementary schools, to start with only two teachers were appointed, one Hindu and one Muslim, and English, Tamil and Telugu were taught. "The object of instructing the children of Mohammedans in Tamil, Telugu and English and of insisting on them to acquire these tongues by hope of reward was to give them means of earning their livelihood in the offices under the Madras Government. The knowledge of these tongues was a test of fitness."[29] But the Government notification guardedly stated, "No preference can be accorded to the pupils of the Nawab's contemplated educational institution in the attainment of employment in the public service. The Government will help him in the administration and choice of competent teachers."[30] The teachers were selected by a committee of three Muslims and two Englishmen. The Nawab's Diwan and the Government agent were ex-officio members of the committee and by them of the other European and Muslim members were chosen with the approval of the Government and the Nawab.[31] Thus by the time the dispatches (Wood's Dispatch) of the Court of Directors of 1854 and 1859 appeared, a good foundation for the education of the Muslims had been laid. These two dispatches outlined the measures to be adopted for the furtherance of the education of Indians.

The Madras Governor Lord Hobart was a person who took keen interest on the Primary Education of the Indians especially of the Muslims. He prepared guidelines to the Municipal chairmen and local bodies in consultation with Educational officers and formed a scheme in 1876. Sufficient grants were allotted and Muslim pupils were required to pay only half of what a Hindu pupil had to pay as school fee. About 125 Maktabs were started in 1877 in the old Madras Presidency with about 2600 pupils. These Maktabs exerted a healthy influence by becoming feeders to the middle school or Madrasas. Almost all Muslim children between 8 and 12 attended the Maktabs, irrespective of their economic condition. Muslim attendance in Maktabs was positively greater than that of Hindu boys in Pyall schools and Patasala's. Speaking about the character and usefulness of Maktabs, Mr. Griegg, the Director of Public Instruction remarked, "*One of the Chief drawbacks to their (Muslim) advancement has been their unwillingness to take advantage of the State System of Education to the same extent as Hindus, if such a course involved the sacrifice of the character of their schools. It is owing to this circumstance that the department has made greater concession to Mohammedan indigenous schools than to Hindu indigenous schools. The policy of the Department was to try generally the mosque or Quran schools capable of doing useful secular work without disturbing the religious basis of the school. This end has been affected by keeping out the Mullah for a secular teacher. It is owing to the adoption of this system that the Mohammedans' education has advanced so fast in the Madras Presidency."*[32] The view that Quran schools served no purpose is debatable. Schools are a means for disciplining the rising young generation. It is not desirable that they should be excluded from the educational system.

Besides Maktabs there were other elementary schools for the Muslim children. The Director of Public Instructions induced certain Muslim teachers with handsome aids to start Elementary schools. Pointing out this purpose the Director of Public instruction said, "This course I adopted with a view to encourage young Mohammedans to join the normal schools and to take up the profession of school master, with the view gradually of creating a number of good Elementary schools."[33]

After pursuing basic religious education in the mosque schools, when they came to the level of High school education and sought admission in Anglo-vernacular schools they were much older than the Hindu boys, whereas the Hindu boys' whole energy was devoted to secular education. The Report of Public Instruction in Madras in 1862-63 pointed out, "The difficulties attended by the Musalman education are much greater than those pertaining to the institutions of Hindus. One of the principal is the advantage at which Musalman lads commenced their studies; another is the number of languages of which it is either necessary or desirable for him to obtain knowledge."[34]

The question of languages in school teaching had always presented special difficulties for Indian Muslims. In fact as Philip Hartog points out, "Perhaps in no other country at the present day do differences of creed and language give rise to such difficulties in the educational system as in India. Nowhere else are the differences so fundamental or on so immense a scale."[35] Language posed a big problem to most of the Muslim pupils because, excepting for the Labbais, their mother tongue was Urdu. It was not the vernacular in any single district. In Muslim schools at the primary and middle school levels Urdu was recognized as the vernacular language and other subjects like arithmetic and geography were taught and examined in Urdu. At the level of the third or fourth standard there was the choice of a second language. In the case of Urdu speaking Muslim pupils it was either English or a vernacular of the district in which the school was located, if the Muslim students had to sit with other students in the general schools. Elucidating this point the acting DPI, Colonel Mac Donald in 1872 remarked, "There are obvious reasons which render it necessary that Mohammedans should be taught in separate schools and classes up to a certain extent, as there is much which can only be learnt and explained through the medium of the vernacular, but when they pass under the charge of European or East Indian masters and secure all instructions through the medium of English they rather gain than lose by being associated with Hindu boys in their studies."[36] The educational policy of the British seems to be to raise the Muslims to the level of Hindus and put them on par with them. A point to be noted here is that the British had to start yet their 'divide and rule' policy in their administration.

There were schools started by private persons exclusively for Muslims. On the other hand the Government also inaugurated Government schools specially intended for Muslims. The Madrasa-i-Azam, which was started in 1851, changed as a Government institution in 1860. With this another Government institution, the Mylapore middle school and Harris school were the only high class institutions originated in a legacy of $1500 by Honourable Sybilla Harris; which handed over to the Church Missionary Society for the establishment of a school for Muslims. In December 1855 the Madras Government sanctioned a handsome donation of Rs. 7000 in aid for the Harris school. The application for the grant stated that it was the first of it kind started for the educational welfare of the Muslim.[37] The school was inaugurated in 1857. But many Muslims did not like to go to Harris school. Muslim newspapers criticized the school as a Christian seminary teaching Bible and converting Muslims to Christianity.[38] A certain student of Harris school was socially ostracized. Moulvis boycotted the Nikkah ceremonies of the Harrisians.[39] A 'Fatwa' (a legal decision of a recognized Muslim jurist or scholar) known as 'Triplicane Fatwa' was issued ex-communicating those who aided and assisted the missionaries of Harris school.[40]

Even after the great efforts taken by the British Government the Muslim boys under instruction throughout the State in the year 1870-71 was 4301 only. In that, majorities were from the primary classes, few were from the middle and matriculation classes. There was hardly any Muslim scholar in a college. The role of Madrasa-I-Azam and Harris school in equipping the Muslim youth for the civil service and the unwillingness of many of the Muslims to take full advantage of the schools was mentioned in the Government records, "During the last thirteen or fourteen years (1858-1871) the Madarasa-I-Azam and the Harris school, both instructions established for the exclusive benefit of Mohammedans, have furnished the Mohammedan youth of the capital with the means of obtaining a good school education and of fitting themselves for the prosecution of those higher studies which are followed in the Presidency College. But not withstanding these advantages only one Muslim boy has become a graduate, only this year. In the list of successful candidates at the special test examinations which are prescribed for all but the lowest appointment in the uncovenanted civil service the number of Mohammedans is lamentably small."[41]

In the Government schools where the Muslims were admitted excepting the Labbais who spoke Tamil, the Urdu speaking Muslims were placed at a great disadvantage because the medium of instruction was either Tamil or Telugu. These drawbacks with the Urdu speaking Muslims and advantage to the Hindus was pointed out by the Proceedings of the Educational Department itself, "The Schools infact were exclusive reference of Hindus, except the case of Madras-I-azam and the Mylapore school, the Mohammedan section of the population was practically ignored in the education arrangements at present in force in the Government schools."[42]

In spite of this drawback in the system of Education the British Government gave a self-appreciation on their achievements in the education field. However, the British Government was proud of their achievement in the field of education. The Government of Madras convened the meeting of the Syndicate of Madras University and asked it to take some measures to attract the Muslim pupils to University education as recommended by the Education Commission of 1882.[43] The facts analysed by the Commission showed that without any doubt the Muslims were trailing behind the Hindus regarding their educational progress.

The attendance of the Muslims in various institutions, Government aided and unaided, as compared with the total attendance in 1881-82, was indicative of their lack of interest in education.[44] There were only four Muslims in Presidency College in the year 1856-57.[45] There were only 7 graduates in 1881-82.[46] There was only one Muslim Doctor of Assistant Surgeon grade and one licentiate in medicine and surgery in 1882.[47] It is interesting to note that one Mohideen Sheriff was such an outstanding person in his knowledge about herbs that he wrote "Materia Medica of Madras" which was a compendium on drugs belonging to the vegetable kingdom. Up to 31st March 1893, 56 graduates had obtained the degree of Master of Arts, no less than 32 of them being Brahmins and only one Muslim, similarly of 7 masters of law 4 were Brahmins and none a Muslim and of 428 Bachelors of Law 312 were Brahmins and only 3 were Muslim. Out of total of 2679 Bachelor of Arts 1836 was Brahmins and 20 Muslims. Again among 53 Bachelors of Engineering 37 were Brahmins and there was not a single Muslim; also of licentiates in teaching 15 were Brahmins and none a Muslim.[48] The status of the higher education of the Muslims as enumerated above undoubtedly proves the deplorable condition.

The Education Commission formed in 1882 by the British Government of India made several sittings at Calcutta and recommended certain measures for the development of the education of the Muslims, which brought a greater change in the condition. Subsequent efforts taken by the Government were purely on the basis of recommendations which were very significant. The Commission gave due importance to the Muslim education and said, "Not merely with regard to justice but with a leaning towards generosity."[49] After a thorough enquiry it found that the Muslims were trailing far behind the rest of the population of India in education as well as in employment. For this the Government could not be blamed. It was due to the negligence of the Muslim community towards education. However the Commission recommended, "The special encouragement of Mohammedan Education is regarded as a legitimate charge on local, on Municipal and on Provincial funds."[50] The Commission recommended to those of the Mohammedan school which were established by Muslim indigenous effort to include the secular subjects in their curriculum.[51] It recommended further to have Urdu or any other language as medium of instruction in Primary and Middle school level as they like. In order to promote the Urdu and Persian languages, provisions were made to allot finance from the public funds to teach those languages. To acquire Higher English education by the Muslims a special attention and effort was made. Special scholarships were instituted for them. Liberal grants-in-aid were sanctioned to the private Muslim educational institutions. Schools and colleges were allowed to be established.[52] The Commission gave due importance to train the Muslims in teaching profession so as to work in the normal schools. Only Muslims were to be appointed as Inspectors of Muslims schools.

A separate section on the education of the Muslims was started in the Annual Report on Public Instruction published by the Government. The Central Government ordered the Provincial Governments to give equal proportion in patronizing the educated Muslims on par with other communities.[53] The Recommendation was generally accepted by the Central and the Provincial Government. The Madras Government made an account of the progress of Muslim education from time to time and devised means for its extension. The Government sought to encourage the education of the Muslim girls by reducing the minimum attendance requirement in Muslim girls' schools. To qualify a Muslim girls' school eligible for grant only an average minimum attendance of eight pupils during the three months preceding the application for grant was required. But with a view to encourage the establishment of private schools for Muslim girls the average minimum attendance was reduced to four in 1884.[54] The Madrasa-I-Azam was reorganized in 1886. A special Deputy Inspector of Muslim schools was appointed whose range included many districts. There was also special Inspecting schoolmaster employed for Muslim school. In 1889, Greigg the Director of Public Instruction recommended a special Inspecting Agency for Muslims. The Government accordingly in 1890, sanctioned the employment of two additional sub assistants Inspectors.[55]

At the close of 1886 there were 508 schools for Muslims of which 8 were Secondary schools 3 Special Education schools and the rest were Primary which together were attended by 15024 Muslim students, only 1065 of them were girls. In 1890, Madras city alone had 7 elementary schools for Muslims 4 in Triplicane, 2 in Royapettah and 1 in Perambur. The Director of Public Instruction proposed to increase the number of schools in Muslim pockets in the capital city like Pudupet, Muthialpet, Chintadaripet, Royapuram etc. There was a demand for increasing the number of schools. The extra cost was estimated at Rs.1900. It was to be met partly from the fee revenue and partly from the lump sum provision of Rs. 2000 in the budget for 1890-91.[56]

The Government of Madras Presidency sanctioned special scholarships for the Muslim students. The scholarships were awarded on the basis of the results of the matriculation, lower secondary and primary examinations. Among these six scholarships were sanctioned to the Muslim students to pursue their degree examinations, there were also scholarships given to the Muslim students in professional colleges.[57] The Madras Government realized that the attention directed towards the improvement of Muslim education and thereby financial help given for those purposes were regarded as lawful expense on the Government exchequer. Local self Governments in the Madras state were ordered to open schools for Muslims. In other forms also exceptional assistance had been rendered to Muslim education. Muslim had long been enjoying the privilege of paying half fee in all public schools and colleges and Muslim student undergoing training for the profession of teaching were given an increased rate of stipend from the provincial fund. Under the Grant-in-aid code all schools for Muslims were treated as poor schools, irrespective of their economic condition.[58]

Regarding the payment of salary to the teachers employed in schools intended for the Muslims a salary Grants system was introduced. The Madrasas were requested to have secular subjects also in their curriculum. The Government accepted that there was no need to fix special standards for Muslim primary schools because they already had their own separate curriculum in Urdu. The principal medium of instruction in primary and middle schools for Muslims was their own mother tongue except in localities where they desired that some other language be adopted. Muslim teachers were employed in Muslim schools. Associations for the promotion of Muslim education were recognized and often consulted. Finally in the disposal of official patronage the claims of Muslims were kept in view and if the proportion of members of the Muslim community in Government service compared unfavorably with that of other communities. It was due to the fact that very few Muslims who offered themselves for employment satisfied the condition of appointment to the public services.[59]

Even after the painstaking efforts by the Government on the Muslims to take up the English education their refusal to oblige to it became the main cause for their backwardness. The reason behind this according to the Muslims was their patriotism, which prevented them to learn English. But contrary to this their progressive minded leaders pointed out that only by learning English and doing things in equal terms will be helpful to them to drive out Britishers. The teaching at the mosques preceded the lesson at the school and often intended up as scholarship in Arabic and Persian whereas for a Hindu the one object was to obtain an education, which would fit him for an official or professional career. "The Mohammedan parent often chooses for his son while at schools an education which will secure for him an honored place among the learned of his own community rather those one which will command success in the modern professions or in official life".[60] The Musalmans had the opinion on the values of Persian and Hindustani education as their heritage. The adherence to this tradition resulted in the number of Muslims employed in Government departments being comparatively small. But they began to realize the need of the hour was Western education. The Muslims' appeal for employment opportunities in the British offices was a good old and present even during the time of the British East India Company. They got some appointments but they were microscopic minority.

The British showed no disparity by birth or creed or caste or colour in giving employment opportunities to their subjects. They decided to give fairer share in the public services to the qualified Musalmans in English education. When the Government wanted the Collectors' report on the implications of the decisions of the Government, the Collectors informed the Government that there were very few qualified Muslims in their respective districts.[61] The Collector of Tanjore informed the Government that there was no application for jobs from any qualified Muslim in the district. The Collector of Madura said that he had not been able to find qualified Mohammedans and did not know where to look for them.[62] Even as late as 1882, there were only 2 Muslim Deputy Collectors out of 45, 2 District Munsiffs out of 40, and 5 Tahsildhars out of 180 each. In the Salt Department and also in the Registration Department there were no Muslims at all.[63] In 1884 in the Department of Education out of 149 officers on salaries over Rs.100 only 2 were Muslims.[64]

In order to do full justice to the demands of the Muslims in the all India basis the Government of India formed a Public Service Commission in 1886, "To do full justice to the claims of natives of India to higher and more extensive employment in public service."[65] In those days Sir Syed Ahamed Khan Bahadur and Khazi Shahabuddin Khan Bahadur were the only two gentlemen who represented the views of the Muslims from the north and south respectively. The grievance of the Muslims of the Madras Presidency was seriously viewed by the Government and the Government welcomed their opinions and grievances to discuss upon, by the Commission. The Commission said in its report, "There are evidences to show that large and important sections of the Mohammedans entertain doubt as to the suitability of open competition as a sufficient test of the possession of Indian candidates of the qualifications necessary for high administrative office and prefer either pure nomination or limited competition among nominated candidates possessed of certain antecedent qualifications...it must of course be remembered that their (Muslims) opinion on such a point can scarcely fail to be influenced by a consciousness of the inability of their co-religionist, as a rule, to compete successfully in purely educational tests with those sections of their fellow countrymen whose progress in education is considerably more advanced than their own."[66] The sub committee appointed to give expert opinion expressed its view that with the improvement of education among the Muslims they would feel more confident and compete with others on equal terms.[67]

The Muslims failed to understand the merits and advantages of western education in the worldly life. They confused themselves in differentiating the British and the western education. Their hesitation to learn English and pursue western education was obvious. Thomas Munro, the Governor of the Madras Presidency remarked on Muslims, "It is easy to find Mohammedan schools and not difficult to make the boys attend but it is impossible to make them learn."[68] The wrong opinions on Western education by the Muslims revealed through a Muslim newspaper: "It is a great cruelty that the English education is forced upon Her Majesty's Indian subjects; there is no pressing necessity for it. Are we going to rule England that we should learn English…it is a sheer waste of time and labour to learn English, especially when we see so many English learned educated persons disrespectful drunkards and utterly wanting in manners."[69]

The merits and advantages of the western education was rightly understood by the Hindu population, in due course more and more learned English and got appointments in the Government services. This resulted to the lagging of Muslims behind the Hindus in all walks of life. The cause of the Muslims' under employment was pointed out by the Education Commission of 1882, "Whilst a radical change was introduced in the Administrative policy of the country rendering it necessary on all aspirants for office under Government to know the language of the rulers no order was making English education compulsory on the contrary up to the year 1864 the Muslim were the *'sine qua non'* for the Government employment or for entering the profession of law. The order of the Government declaring the candidates for Munshiffs and leaderships may pass their examination either in Urdu or in English remained as late as 1864. A year or two later, however a sudden change was introduced upsetting the previous order and declaring that English alone should be the language in which the reexaminations for higher grade leadership and Munshiffs should be held. The measures since used from time to time placed the Muslims under a complete disadvantage. Before they had quite awakened to the necessity of learning English, they were shut out from Government employments."[70]

After a great trial and ordeal the Muslims slowly understood their crucial condition. There was a slow change in their attitude and behavior on Western education. The Nawab Wallajah, as requested by one of his relatives named Amjad Ali, appealed to the Government to sanction aid to start a school. Further the Nawab pointed out, "To teach the Muslims English language, only the ignorant people consider it as prohibited and against their religion."[71] The Mohammedan Education Association of Salem declared with a nationalistic and rationalistic view, "Our nation has ceased to maintain her glorious traditions through the neglect of education, especially English. If we continue as lethargic in the future as we are in the present, the world will soon close its doors against us. We must therefore all join in earnest effort to raise our nation from the abyss of ignorance into which she has fallen. We are on board the same ship and if the ship is wrecked we shall all, high and low, sink together. We must therefore rise ourselves that the ship shall not be wrecked".[72] This declaration echoed the feelings of the Muslims in the Madras Presidency. Following this there was an appreciable change and progress in Muslim students' strength throughout the Presidency especially in Thanjavur and Trichinopoly.[73]

In order to accommodate eligible Muslim candidates in the Government Services the Commission recommended, "There must be a proportion fixed by Government of officials in each department according to the proportion of the people of all persuasions, Hindus, Christians and Muslims...unless some such restriction is imposed it is hopeless to expect either Eurasians, Europeans or Muslims to contest on equal terms with the Hindus whose progress at school or colleges is ordinarily more rapid than either of the above classes, whilst they can afford to sell their services cheaper, at any rate than Eurasians and Europeans."[74] The Muslim press namely

Mazhar-ul-Ajaib already voiced about the proportional representations.[75]

The Government had decided and tried proportional representation for the Muslims on a limited scale. They found their experience frustrating in civil subordinate service. In Medical Department the fact that "Government have resolved to afford exceptional temporary advantages for a term of 5 years, to candidates of the Mohammedan community by reserving certain number of appointments for them"[76] and it further said "One fifth of the ninety five candidates required will accordingly be reserved for competition among Mohammedan matriculation candidates." But with one solitary exception no Muslim responded and the appointments reserved for them were filled by youths of other communities. It was remarkable that Brahmins discarding their caste prejudices and traditional apathy to the profession of medicine came forward in large numbers to take up the appointments. On the contrary the Muslims stuck in their traditional attitudes, failed to circumstances. A competitive examination of any kind was anathema to them. The Surgeon General wrote to the Chief Secretary to Government, "It will be seen that it is not for want of inducement that Mohammedan young men have not availed themselves of the appointments reserved for them."[77] It is therefore not surprising that the Government decided to appoint foreign Muslim nationals in Public Service.[78]

Contribution of Muslim Press to the Promotion of Muslim Education at the Close of the Nineteenth Century

In the nineteenth century newspapers were the only media available to expose things. In that respect the press had played a significant role in bringing education closer to the people. As such the Muslim papers and magazines did a yeoman service to the cause of the Muslim education. They invited the attention of the Government on particular problem, subjects, complaints etc. and appeal to the Government for rectification. The Government also gave its ear to the grievances often put forwarded by the newspapers.

The editor of 'The Mohammedan' offered to publish advertisements about the vacancies in the Government services on free of cost. This offer was communicated to all the departments by the Government.[79] The Muslim associations requested the Government to inform them about the opportunities available to the Muslims so as to make the news reach the Muslim youth. They watched the progress of the Muslim community in every field.[80]One of the causes of the illiteracy of Muslims in India was rightly pointed out by the Urdu paper 'Shamsul Akhbar' that illiteracy of India especially of Mohammedans was mainly due to the use in education a difficult foreign language i.e. English. It declared that a language like Hindustani (mostly Urdu) should be adopted as a Common Instructional Vernacular of India.[81]

The Anjuman-i-Islam of Salem (A Muslim Association) presented a Memorandum to the Government of Madras and gave statistical information about the increase in the number of vacancies in the public services to the Muslims. In response to the memorandum the Chief Secretary remarked, "The Muslims must help themselves. They can work if they like. It is this failure to put their heart into it that is the chief, if not the only cause of their not obtaining better appointments and more of them. They have the same facilities as other races have and if they do not choose to avail themselves of that it is their own outlook."[82] The Muslims of Madura submitted a memorandum and also a proposal, which was approved by the Government. Interestingly the proposal included educating women folk in handicrafts to earn their livelihood.[83] They also requested for a special concession to Muslims' education and employment in proportion to their population.

They bothered least about the social, economic, political and historical disparity in them and scheduled castes. "For the advancement of scheduled castes the Government has found it necessary to accord special help to them until they are able to help themselves and though the Muslim community forms a large proportion of Her Majesty's subjects yet it is not able to improve its conditions and maintain its position against other classes."[84] In answer to the memorandum the Chief Secretary replied, "What is needed is not so much an addition to the already liberal concessions made by the Government as an exhibition on the part of the Muslim community of a greater desire to take advantage to the full of these concessions."[85] Lord Connemera, the Governor of Madras in his address to the Anjuman-I-Islam of Dindigul on 26th October 1887, pointed out, "If any class has obtained a larger share of public employment than others it is owing entirely to its own energy and ability, and it is quite with in the power of the Muslim community to distinguish themselves in this respect."[86]

Regarding the appointment of British people as inspecting staff for various Mohammedan schools in the Presidency a resolution was moved by one Zynulabidin. In his resolution he pointed out that Mohammedan community should be given this privilege, which is enjoyed by the Europeans and also added that a much smaller community than the Mohammedans in the Presidency was unlawfully enjoying it[87]. This resolution was accepted later and Muslim inspectors were appointed. Like-wise establishment of technical schools, factories in Madras were also demanded by the Muslims.[88] As a service to the community the Muslim newspapers for example Anjuman-I-Mufidi-Ahle-Islam furnished in their papers with information regarding the employment opportunities in the Government services, helped to write Public Service Examinations, information about the Government concessions were also given to the Muslim community.[89]

Contribution of Associations and Organizations to the Cause of Muslim Education at the Close of Nineteenth Century

Even though, 'suppression, divide and rule' was the common policy of the British they never opposed to the formation of associations and organizations for the welfare of the people. The Mohammedans Educational Association of Salem was formed in 1895. The Salem Collector Stokes cooperated with the association and did great service to the Muslims' informal education. The Anjumen-I-Mufide-Ahle Islam of Madras established by Col. Underwood, paymaster of Carnatic stipends in 1895 collected a fund of Rs. 17,000 for the establishment of a workshop and technical school, an equal amount was contributed by the government to gather within the building grant.[90] It established many workshops employing a number of Muslim boys, men and young men even Ghosha-women. These measures brought a dramatic change in their life. It helped the Muslim women to have some sort of economic independence[91]. The trades carried on in the workshops were carpentry, tailoring and cane work for furniture. The achievements of the Anjuman-I-Mufidi-Ahle Islam hit the headlines of the English newspapers.[92]

On seeing the interest shown by the Associations the Government also sanctioned substantial grants to the Technical Institutes started by the Muslims at Veerarasapuram, Tirunelveli.[93] The central Anjumen, Madras, acted as an employment agent and the Muslims who sought employment were directed by the Government to get their names registered with the Anjuman.[94] The representations were normally relevant to Muslims all over India. The Muslims never failed to acknowledge gratefully the service rendered by Englishmen for their upgradation.[95] Thus by the efforts of the Associations cooperation and mutual understanding developed between the Muslims and the British.

Further, steps were also taken on the recommendations of the associations by the Madras Government in improving the condition of the education of the Muslims. The Government formed a separate 'Board of Mohammedan education' in Madras in 1893. Mr. C.S. Crole appointed as the president to find out further measures to improve the Muslim education. Haji Mir Humayun Bahadur Jah, Col. T.O.W Wood, Mohamed Mahmud Khan Bahadur, Hasamuddin Sahib Bahadur and Waljee Laljee Sait were the other members of the Board.[96] Despite taking these measures the Board became inactive in due course. Khadar Nawaz Khan Bahadur, inspired by the Aligarh Oriental Anglo-Mohammedan College, brought prominent officials, non officials and affluent businessmen among the Muslims from all over India to contribute liberally towards establishing Technical institutions with hostel facilities.[97] The Government allowed him to do all sorts of works except rising funds because the Government servants were not permitted to involve in such activities.[98] The Mohammedan literary society of Madras, another welfare organization of the Muslims, was contributing its mite to the educational and intellectual welfare of the Muslims.[99]

The various Muslim Associations in the country appealed to the Government for special relaxation in Examinations and employment rules for the Muslims. Such demands were also made by suppressed castes and tribes but there was a basic difference between their demands. The Harijans were suppressed people for generations, whereas the Muslims were once ruling class and lawmakers. The Muslims thought that they were deprived of those privileges by the British rule. In the early stage their attitude and demands were different from the rest of the society. Nevertheless, some of their demands showed their weakness and their failure to understand the English education in proper prospects.

The Ahle-i-Islam of Salem represented to the Government for relaxation of rules in the pleaders Examination so that more Muslims could be appointed as pleaders. The representation said, "Great inconveniences and utmost difficulties are experienced by us for want of a competent English knowing Mohammedan first grade Pleader to practice in the tribunals and to represent us in the Judicial matter... the passing of pleaders test has of late been difficult so much so that none amongst our class is likely for the present to be employed as pleader of the first grade owing to the paucity of graduates."[100] To the great disappointment of the association its demands were rejected totally by the Government. A descendant of Nawab Wallejah, one Mohammedan Abdul Khader appeared for matriculation examination and failed many times in History and Geography. He appealed to Lord Wenlock, the Governor for relaxation of rules and exemption from any examination qualifying for employment in public service. Incompetency and unreasonableness could not have gone further.[101]

The prominent Muslim leaders raised their voice in the Legislature and asked the Government to give an account of the measures taken for the development of Muslim education. They also suggested the Government to divert Wakf funds to education, to reserve appointments in each department for the eligible Muslim candidates.[102] The Muslims' incapability to compete with other communities made them envy upon their rivals and began to boast of their noble birth. The editor of Majharul-Ajaif remarked, "As long as Hindus and half castes hold high appointments in Public Service there is no chance of giving a lift to Mohammedans...there were some offices in which the Mohammedans are rarely employed not withstanding their merits and noble birth, whereas in the case of the half caste, however mean his origin may be, preference is given to him simply because he is dressed as an European."[103] Their utter lack of understanding of the changed situation and their diehard conservatism are evident in the following lines in Jarida-I-Razgar, a popular Muslim Newspaper. It is deeply to be experienced that all is preferable to an Aalim, a scholar in Arabic and Persian, and is nominated to act as Pleader in the Court of Justice, whereas the latter is debarred from holding the post of Munsiff."[104]

The Examination system was scorned and the value of experience for a prospective Government servant was praised by the Editor of Miratul-Ara. He complained, "Experience and ability are noting to the Government compared with test of Examination, old and experienced men are discarded for youth who have passed only the name of an examination in our opinion an experience ignoramus is at least equal to a clever Tyro."[105]

A community asking for more privileges and concessions in due course would lead them to inactiveness. The fear of the Muslims to protect them from the rest of the population was a misunderstanding. One of the members of the Education Commission of 1882, pointed out, "It would be an unmixed gain if the Mohammedans came forward and qualified themselves to take a larger and more important share in the administration of the country; but the improvement must, and I believe, will come from their own effort. No attempt to improve their position by protecting them against the competition of other classes can have permanently beneficial effect."[106] This sort of mendicancy made a Deputy Inspector of Schools named Mohammed Razak Khan to declare before the Madras Provincial Committee of Education. "I must raise my voice in Muslim's interest against the miscalled liberality and wholesome concessions made them in certain instances by the relaxation of rules. I hold that favour to Muslims may take any other form than this, which I deem to be most pernicious to and distractive of their real interest. The Muslim who would seek to evade a prescribed general test of competency, in my opinion, would deserve nothing."[107] But his opinion was not given any importance by the Muslims.

In spite of such criticism, the majority of the Muslims favoured protection and asked for it. Taking the opinions of some of the expert administrators who knew very well the Muslims persuaded the Government to follow a policy of discouragement and refusing the applications of the Muslims for special concessions and some sort of relaxation in matter of employment. However the Government relaxed the rules on petty issues. The letter of the Secretary to the Government of India recommending the name of a Muslim for the post of Deputy Collector shows the Government's attitude to the Question of Muslims in Public Service. The Secretary said, "As this Government attaches the utmost importance to opening up a promising career to Mohammedan gentlemen they would very strongly urge the appointment of their nominees not withstanding that his age now slightly exceeds the prescribed limit."[108] When conditions changed the need for Western education had been realized by the Muslim community. The strict policy of the Government also induced the spirit of the Muslims to compete with other communities in equal terms.

The spread and the significance of Western education were first realized by North Indian Muslims. The intellectual and religious awakening movements for such purpose were started in the North seeking religious and social reforms. Such movements and awakening were rarely found among the South Indian Muslims. In North India, the Hindus were the first people to demand for socio-religious, intellectual reforms. However, this affected also the Muslims of the North also. In 1885, in the city of Lahore, the Anjuman-i-Himayat-i-Islam, i.e. the "Society for the Defence of Islam" was started. In 1894 "Nadwat-ul-Ulama" or Society of Muslim Theologians was started in Lucknow. Because of the efforts of these movements an intellectual awakening and a demand for socio-religious reform sprang up. But such changes were very less in the South. However, the branches of movements in the North were also started in the South, which worked for the development of social, religious and educational conditions of the Muslims.[109]

Like the mediaeval age the interferences of religious elites were also found when the Western Education was introduced in India among the Muslims. They said to the people that reading English jeopardize their religious faith and culture. The British tried their best to convince the vainglorious and conservative Muslims in studying the English education. In the beginning, the Muslims were very much scared of the British approach and followed a defensive attitude against the educational changes introduced by the British Government. They failed to notice the Hindu advancement and the Muslim lagging behind in all fields. In spite of these efforts by the Government and the elite Muslims, the Muslim folks remained unchanged and unmoved. The Muslims' overwhelming love for traditional Madarasa education and religious values forbid them to accept the Western Education. For this condition prevailing among them, the Muslims had to blame themselves only. Lack of philanthropic munificence, missionary zeal and self-initiative of the society were the sole cause for their backwardness.

The change of time advancement of science and other factors made the Muslims rethink over their beliefs and attitudes. They also witnessed the progress of the other communities in government services and other walks of life. They realized the indispensability of the Western education in the progress of socio-economic, political and employment opportunities. Because of this realization and the change of attitude of the Muslims there was an appreciable improvement in the education towards the end of the nineteenth century. The unhealthy reaction of the Muslims begins to vanish gradually. The Muslims understood that Western education is a historical necessity and it did not recommend unhealthy personal habits or antipathy to the common people. Individual liberty, social equality, collective progress, reason as the supreme criterion to judge ideas and institutions, intense nationalism etc. are some of the good ideas found in Western education. Thus the Muslims decided to prefer Modernism and to end Mediaevalism.

REFERENCES

1. *Selection from Educational Records*, Part I, 1781-1839, p. 7. Tamil Nadu Archives. (T.N.A.).
2. *Report of the Education Commission, 1882*, Part III, p. 483, T.N.A.
3. *Ibid.*, p. 483.
4. *Ibid.*, p. 484.
5. *Ibid.*, p. 485.
6. *Ibid.*, p. 485.
7. *Ibid.*, p. 486.
8. *Ibid.*, p. 486.

9. *Ibid.*, p. 487.

Race	Entrance			First Arts		
	Examined	Passed	% of passed to examined	Examined	Passed	% of passed to examined
Brahmans	2150	670	31.2	486	295	60.7
Hindus not Brahmans	1006	290	27.2	173	86	49.7
Musalmans	71	19	26.8	10	6	60.0

10. *BRC 1828*, Vol. 1133, p. 415, T.N.A.

Representation of the Indian Education Commission 1882

Class of Instructions	Total Number of students	Musalmans	%
College English	1669	30	1.7
College-oriental	30	...	...
High School English	4836	117	2.4
Middle School English	18553	723	3.8
Middle School Vernacular	511	2	0.4
Primary School English	63295	4973	7.8
Primary School Vernacular	76983	19232	6.9
High School English Girls	2	...	...
Middle School English Girls	190	...	...
Middle School Vernacular Girls	197	1	0.5
Primary School English Girls	1897	...	...
Primary School Vernacular Girls	18468	427	2.3
Normal Schools for Masters	799	42	5.2
Normal School for Mistress	157	...	...
Total	**387597**	**25547**	**6.5**

11. *BRC 1830*, Vol. 1246, p. 7840, T.N.A.

12. *Census of Madras Town, Report on the Result of the Educational Census of Madras*, November 1871, p. 13, T.N.A.

13. Penny Frank, *The Church in Madras*, Vol. III, p. 254.
14. Imam Zaffer, *Muslims in India*, 1975, p. 202.
15. Hampton, H.V., *Biographical Studies in Modern Indian Education*, 1947, p. 213.
16. *Report of the Education Commission, 1882,* Part II, p. 483, T.N.A.
17. Bishop Caldwell, *Reminiscence*, p. 83.
18. Farquhar, *Modern Religious Movement in India*, New Delhi, 1929, p. 91.
19. Hunter, W.W., *The Indian Musalmans,* 1871, p. 149.
20. *Ibid.,* p. 174.
21. Thomas P.J., *The Growth of Higher Education in Southern India*, p. 36.
22. *Selections from the Educational Records*, Part I, 1781-1893, *Minutes of Sir Thomas Munro*, T.N.A.
23. Pub.cons.Vol-576, pp. 3724-28, *Petition of the Muslim Inhabitants of Trichy to M.J.Rawlinson*, Secretary to Public Instruction, 6th October 1829, T.N.A.
24. Pub.Cons.vol.571, p.1007, *Letter from the Chief Secretary to the Board for the College and Public Instruction to the Chief Secretary to the Government* dated 13th February 1829, T.N.A.
25. Pub.Cons., Vol. 476, *Proceedings of FSG*, 19th November 1830, p. 2774, T.N.A.
26. *Selections from the Records of the Madras Government*, No.XLI, part-II, *Report on Applicant of Grants-in-aid of Schools Unconnected with the Government*, p. 64, T.N.A.
27. Pol.Cons.1851, Vol. 494, p. 2295, *Letter from Nawab's Secretary Mohamed Ali to Balfour Agent at Chepauk,* dated 22nd March 1851, T.N.A.
28. *Ibid.*
29. *Letter from E.G.Balfour, Assistant Surgeon, Girl's Bodyguard to Major Garstin*, Government Agent at Chepauk, dated 26th September 1850, T.N.A.
30. No.183, Political Department, *Extract from the Minutes of Consultation*, dated 29th April 1851, T.N.A.
31. Balfour Edward, *Carnatic Stipendiary of 1801* (Madras 1858), p.370, T.N.A.

32. *No.319-320, Educational 14th April, 1892*, Letter from Greigg, DPI to the Chief Secretary, dated 29th March 1892, T.N.A.
33. *No.80, Educational (misc)* 19th February 1883, *No.704, Educational (misc)* 19th October 1883, T.N.A.
34. *Report on Public Administration in the Madras Presidency for 1862-63*, Para II, p. 32, T.N.A.
35. Hartog, Philip, *Some Aspects of Indian Education, Past and Present*, p. 48
36. *No.288, Proceedings of the Government of Madras in the Education Department*, dated 7th October 1872, T.N.A.
37. *Report on Public Instruction in Madras Presidency for the Year 1855-56.* Para 79, T.N.A.
38. *Shamsul-Akbar*, 17th April 1876.
39. *Jalva-E-Sakhum*, 15th April 1888.
40. *Jarida-I-Rozgar*, 14th June, 1884.
41. *No.288, Proceedings of the Government of Madras, Educational Department*, dated 7th October 1872, T.N.A.
42. *Ibid.*
43. *Report of the Education Commission of 1882*, Part II, p.484, T.N.A.
44. *Ibid.*, p. 484.
45. *Report on Public Instruction in Madras Presidency*, 1856-57, T.N.A.
46. *Administrative Report of the Madras Presidency*, 1881-82, p.195, T.N.A.
47. *No. 66, Letter from Surgeon General W.R.Cornish to the Chief Secretary to Government of Madras* dated FSG, 14th February 1882, T.N.A.
48. *Manual of Standing Information for the Madras Presidency 1893*, Chapter VIII, p.106, T.N.A.
49. *Report on the Education Commission of 1882*, Part II, p.505, T.N.A.
50. *Ibid.*
51. *Ibid.*
52. *Ibid.*

53. *Report on the Education Commission of 1882*, Part II, p. 506, T.N.A.
54. *G.O. No.167, Educational*, 20th June 1884, T.N.A.
55. *Report on Public Instruction in Madras Presidency for 1885-86*, p. 108, T.N.A.
56. *Administration Report of Madras Presidency, 1885-86*, Summary Section VII, p. 42, T.N.A.
57. *Manual of the Administrative of Madras Presidency*, Vol. I, p. 597, T.N.A.
58. *Ibid.*
59. *Report on Public Instructions in the Madras Presidency*, 1900, Vol. I, p. 597, T.N.A.
60. *Report of the Education Commission of 1882*, Part II, p. 505, T.N.A.
61. *No.288, Educational*, 7th October 1872, *No. 87, Revenue*, 19th February 1873, T.N.A.
62. *Proceedings of the Board of Revenue*, 27th August 1873, p. 5382, T.N.A.
63. *Appendix to Education Commission Report*, 1884, p. 277, T.N.A.
64. *Proceedings of the Sub Committee, Public Service Commission Education Department, 1886*, p.109, T.N.A.
65. *G.O No.34/1573-83, (Home Department)* dated 4th October and 42/1859-98 dated 4th November 1886, T.N.A.
66. *Report of the Public Service Commission, 1886-87*, Chapter-I, p. 66, T.N.A.
67. *Proceedings of the Sub Committee, Public Service Commission, 1886*, p.116, T.N.A.
68. *No.67, Quoted in a Letter from H.B.Greigg, DPI to the Chief Secretary of Govt.*, Ootacamund, dated 13th June 1882, T.N.A.
69. *Mazhur-ul-Ajaib*, 8th February 1883, Durab Mohamed Hussain, *Tholughai Ranjita Alangaram,* Dindigul, 1897.
70. *No. 287, Judicial*, 22nd March 1882, T.N.A.
71. *No. 557, Educational*, 6th October 1897, T.N.A.
72. *No.198, Educational*, 2nd April 1897, T.N.A.

73. *Ibid.*
74. *Proceedings of the Sub-Committee of Public Service Commission*, 1887, p.117, T.N.A.
75. *Mazhar-ul-Ajaib*, 21st February 1881.
76. *No.1031, Public*, 23rd September 1882, T.N.A.
77. *Ibid.*
78. *No. 192, Public*, 29th March 1882 Extract of the Proceedings of Government of India in the Home Department (Public) under date, Fort William, 20th March, 1882, T.N.A.
79. *No. 100, Public*, 4th February 1897, T.N.A.
80. *No. 239, Educational*, 23rd April 1897, T.N.A.
81. *Fortnightly Report*, for the second half of October 1926.
82. *No. 29, Educational*, 19th January 1891, T.N.A.
83. *No. 239, Educational (misc)*, 12th April 1893, T.N.A.
84. *Ibid.*
85. *Ibid.*
86. *Speeches of Lord Connemera*, 26th October 1887, p.156.
87. *Andhra Patrika*, Madras, 3rd April 1914.
88. *Jarida-I-Rozgar*, Madras, 28th April 1914.
89. *Anjuman-I-Mufidi-Ahle-Islam*, 2nd May 1914.
90. *No. 77, Educational*, 8th February 1896, T.N.A.
91. *No. 648, Political*, 17th August 1887, T.N.A.
92. *Madras Mail*, Saturday, 28th May 1887.
93. *No. 635, Educational*, 12th October 1889, T.N.A.
94. *No. 202, Educational*, 13th April 1893, T.N.A.
95. *No. 832, Public (misc)*, 26th July 1899, *No.1136, Public (misc)*, T.N.A.
96. *No. 3-9, Educational*, 27th May 1893, *No.441, Educational* 28th June 1893, T.N.A.
97. *No. 197, Educational*, 31st March 1896, T.N.A.
98. *Ibid.*
99. *No. 832, Public (misc)*, 9th October, 1899

100. *No.948, Judicial*, 2nd May 1887. T.N.A.
101. *No.757, Educational*, 6th October 1894, T.N.A.
102. *No.323, Public*, 14th March, 1899, *No.1401, Public*, 22nd December, 1899, *No.630, Public*, 9th June, 1899, *No.1047, Public*, 23rd December, 1899, *No.1940, Judicial*, 13th December, 1898, T.N.A.
103. *Majharul-Ajaib*, 21st February 1881.
104. *Jarida-I-Rozgar*, 8th April 1882.
105. *Miratul-Ara*, 20th July 1874.
106. *Report of the Education Commission of 1882*, Part II, p.605, T.N.A.
107. *Appendix to Education Commission Report*, 1884, p.277, T.N.A.
108. *No.1353-54, Public (Confidential)*, 5th October 1881, T.N.A.
109. Farquhar, *Modern Religious Movements in India*, New Delhi, 1929, p. 350.

3

CHAPTER

British Efforts and the Muslim Response between A.D. 1901 and A.D. 1947

The Muslim community realized the indispensability of the Western education, which made them react and respond to the Government efforts for the progress of their education. Thus, by 1901 A.D onwards, special attention of the British Government directed towards the development of the education of the Muslims of the Madras Presidency gained momentum. A discussion on the British Government's efforts and response of the Muslim community for the improvement of their educational condition between 1901 and 1947 forms the subject matter of this Chapter.

The dawn of the twentieth century marked a great political turmoil and unrest in India. This was further worsened by the reactionary regime of Lord Curzon. His Viceroyalty affected the Educational Development in India particularly the efforts in this regard by the private enterprises. He brought many changes and control in the sphere of education especially in the higher education. The Laissez Faire system of education emphasized by the Woods Despatch of 1854 and further recommended by the 1882 Education Commission was given up. Lord Curzon feared that the Universities were seedbeds of revolutionary ideas. So, he reversed the policy of promotion of education by the private efforts. He began to follow a policy of "Efficiency first expansion next."[1]

The liberalization of Education Policy by the British Government during the later half of the nineteenth century was viewed with distaste by Lord Curzon as it resulted in the alteration of Government policies. Therefore, Curzon planned to reform the educational structure by officializing Indian education through strict norms. To remove these hurdles implemented during the Lord Curzon's regime a resolution was passed by the British Government in the year 1913.[2] Apart from these changes initiated by the Government, non-officials like G.K. Gokhale also moved a Bill to make elementary education free and compulsory. All these changes had a great impact on the growth of education during these two decades. The strict and stringent measures of Lord Curzon brought a fear among the people to start private educational institutions. He appointed a Committee under Thomas Raleigh. Thus, Curzon's reforms were the excessive officialization of the University administration, as a sequel to his apprehension that the Universities were places where the anti British revolutionists sprang up. Higher Education in universities and colleges aimed at dissemination of knowledge and training for life and also an intellectual service to the community at large. But, the higher education in Madras Presidency was not well developed; there were 43 colleges and a University.[3]

The Mohammedan Educational Endowments Committee of Calcutta, which met on to discuss generally the condition of the education of the Muslims in India in 1888, became an occasion to represent that there were numerous endowed properties scattered throughout India to be accumulated and regulated. It pointed out the pitiable condition of the Education of the Muslims of India was mainly due to lack of fund and recommended in its report to the Secretary to the Government of Bengal that those numerous Endowment properties scattered throughout India might be applied to promote the education of the Muslims. It requested the Government to amend the law on endowments so as to make use of the endowment properties to the cause of the promotion of the education of the Muslims and further requested the Government to spend the continuous income from those properties for building schools and improving the infrastructure of the educational institutions.[4] But this recommendation was not examined and considered by the Government. Had this request of the Mohammedan Educational Endowment Committee of Calcutta been accepted and given effect, the education of the Muslims would have had progressed some fifty years in advance, because of the lack of fund was one of the causes for the trailing behind of the Muslims in education The Muslims had to either accept the Governmental concession shown on them or to stand on their own effort to improve their condition.

The Condition of the Education of the Muslims, The Christians and the Hindus in the Beginning of the Twentieth Century

A comparative study on the three religious groups in the beginning of the twentieth century will reveal the educational condition of the Muslims in the Madras Presidency in relation to communities An analysis on these three religious groups based on the Administrative Reports, Director of Public Instructions Records and Census of India Records (between 1891 and 1900) available in the Madras archives will be an useful exercise in this regard.

The following tables show the proportionate increase of English literacy at the close of 1900-1901.

Table 3.1

Religion	Literates (of both sexes) per mille (10,000)		
	10–15	15–20	20 and over
All Religion	72	107	103
Hindu	69	102	99
Mohammedan	66	111	134
Christian	202	271	211

Table 3.2

Religion	Increase per mile (10,000) literates of Both sex		
	10–15	15–20	20 and over
All Religion	290	316	277
Hindu	298	307	267
Mohammedan	297	361	319
Christian	254	377	375

One would naturally expect the proportion of literates in English per mille (i.e. 10, 000) at the period '20 and over' to be greater than such proportion at the earlier age-periods. But if the proportionate increase at the final age-period exceeds that of the earlier period, it is a sign that an uneducated generation is growing up. Happily every indication is in the other direction. The figures noted in the margin show that the younger generations were more than holding positions especially in the Hindu and Christian communities. Even in the case of Mohammedans it is not an unfair supposition that a trading community may seek its education at a later age than those which supply recruits to the clerical and learned profession.[5]

The figures in the below table 3.3 showing proportionate increase at the various periods of age are also encouraging. They may be quoted, while in view of the special importance of female education, similar statements for the sex alone deserve a place.

Statement B, It is true, hardly bears out our contention literally, but then if things are seldom quite so fair as one would wish them to be, here they are quite sufficiently fair to encourage the hope that they will yet be fairer.[6]

Thus, for education taken as but the equivalent of literacy, progress in secondary, or higher education, is difficult to estimate; selection of data on which to found an examination

Table 3.3

Religions	Statement A Female literates per mille (10,000)			Statement B Increase per mille (10,000) female literates		
	10 – 15	15 – 20	20 and over	10 – 15	15 – 20	20 and over
All Religions	22	29	14	514	609	616
Hindu	18	24	11	626	690	712
Mohammedan	16	19	13	408	445	393
Christian	160	211	118	250	427	418

is a matter on which no two persons are likely to agree. So, the recorded results of literacy in English, statistics supplied by the Registrar of Books and those to be found in the University calendars for the decade 1891-1900 is taken for analysis.[7]

There is nothing in particular meritorious in knowledge of English *per se:* (of the Madras Presidency in 1901) the weird reasoning of the northern fellow countrymen occasionally casts up such knowledge as a reproach to the Madrasi; still, there would seem to be a greater educational possibilities in knowledge of two languages than that of one; in Madras in particular, knowledge of English affords opportunity for the commerce and interchange of ideas throughout the Presidency as a whole, as well as beyond its limits. The positive spread of this knowledge is not so far very great; it is claimed but by 66 per 10,000 of the total population; by 53 Hindu and 46 Mohammedans of a similar number. Christians, whose community includes many to whom English is the ordinary means of communication, naturally outstripped all other religions with 541 per 10,000. This Department of Education, as one would expect, is almost entirely confined to one sex. Of some 19 million Hindu, and one and a half million Mohammedan women, but 3,770 and 194 respectively can read and write English. Among Christians, female literates in English numbered 23,124 out of a total of 6,13,280; but it must be admitted that the major portion of this total (14,152) belongs to the European and Anglo-Indian communities.[8]

Table 3.4

Nature of Increase	All Religions	Hindu	Mohammedan	Christian
Absolute	84,784	67,222	4,828	12,469
Per Mille	442	515	613	236

Proportional figures (in the table above) deduced from absolute figures, in which one term is exceedingly great or exceedingly small, are apt to prove misleading. The marginal statement shows the progress, both absolute and proportional, made during the decade 1891-1901 in English literacy.

The table below shows the position of English Education by age periods before 1900 and the marginal statement shows the relation of these figures to those of 1901.

Table 3.5

(Increase per mille - 10,000)

Age Periods	All Religions	Hindu	Mohammedan	Christian
0 – 10	– 40	–29	404	–68
10 – 15	178	246	360	15
15 – 20	374	421	431	226
20 and over	525	598	697	309

It is a permissible supposition that the proportional decrease at the first age period in all religions, and in each religion save Mohammedanism, is due to more accurate enumeration. The absolute figures in the case of Mohammedanism are so small, (an increase from 99 to 139), as to be negligible.

Table 3.6

(Increase per mille - 10,000)

Class dealt with	All Religions	Hindu	Mohammedan	Christian
Literates	284	278	322	339
Literates in English	442	515	613	236

A comparison of the progress of literacy in English with literacy in general may be exhibited for what it is worth.[9] Due to non-availability of correct data and statistical points it is not possible to bring out the comparison.

From the above-mentioned comparative analysis of the three religious groups Hindus, Mohammedans and Christians it is presumed that the analysis shows that the increase at the final age period of the education in English has a positive and encouraging trend.

The special importance of female education deserves the similar state of affairs exhibiting the same positive and encouraging upward trend. Statement B does not show an increasing trend in literacy.

Education taken, as an equivalent of literacy does not reflect the progress made in both secondary and higher education; for which the statistics found in Books of Registrar of have been taken for analysis. Knowledge of two languages offered better and more opportunities than one language. Of all the members of religious community the Christians enjoy a better status with 541 members out of 10,000 with the English language followed by Hindus; only about 53 and Mohammedans with 46, out of 10,000.

As regards the women's education, 3770 out of 19 million Hindu women and 194 out of 1/2 million Mohammedan women can read and write English, whereas 23,124 Christian women out of total 61,328 were literate in English, which include European and Anglo Indian Community. The proportionate figures are quite misleading where the marginal statement refer to the progress made in English literacy.

The subsidiary shows the English education by age period and the relation of the figures in 1901. The Proportion of decrease in all religion except Mohammedanism is shown through accurate enumeration and the absolute figures of Mohammedanism are too negligible to demand any attention.

Among the three religious groups the Christians excel the other two religious groups in the literacy of English. The Christian women were also better in English literacy than their counter parts in the other two religious groups. Although the progress of the Muslims was so small, their enthusiasm to learn English was gradually increasing. The Census of India of 1891 records shows that the Musalman females produced the next best results, though a long interval separates them from their Christian sisters. It is a common belief that Muslims are not so well educated as Hindus but this is erroneous.[10] This statistics, however, refers only to elementary level; in higher level the ratio was not proved due to lack of correct statistics and data.

The statistics of education in the age period for Hindus, Muslims and Christians, some anomalies are found in the Hindu and Muslim figures as in these for whole population, comparatively low proportion of the illiterate among the adult males especially marked in the case of Muslims. According to the Census of India 1891 records, among the males of 20 and over age period, 71 per cent of the Christians, 76 per cent of the Muslims and 82 per cent of the Hindus were illiterate. Among the women, 20 and over age period 9 percent of the Christians, 1.25 per cent of the Muslims and only 0.5 per cent of the Hindus were literate.[11]

Even though the educational policy from the time of Curzon aimed at checking unrestricted growth of standards, in fact during Curzon's period, there was a comparative increase of students and improvement of standards in schools. Thus qualitative rather than quantitative improvement was perceptible in secondary instruction, during this period. Grants were granted under Grant-in-Aid system to the various Schools and Colleges.[12]

Unmindful of the restrictions and tight control of the British Government, the Muslim Philanthropists and progressive minded leaders took efforts to improve the educational condition of their society. An All India Muslim Educational Conference was held at Madras in 1901 due to the efforts of the Muslim leaders.[13] The main aim of this Conference firstly, was to bring awareness among the Muslim mass towards western education. Secondly, the conference tried to bring the attention of the British Government on the education of the Muslims. This was a first and a major attempt of the Muslim community towards their educational development in the Madras Presidency. This effort even though was not very successful; definitely affected some sort of inclining attitude among the Muslims towards the English education. But unfortunately this change of attitude of the Muslim community was not encouraged during the time of Lord Curzon's administration.

The growth of the education of the Muslims was not steady and uniform. There was periodic increase and decrease in the expansion of the western education among the Muslims of Madras Presidency. The total number of schools increased in a year subsequently decreased in the next year and the pupils' strength under instruction also was in the same condition. On studying the Administrative Reports, the Director of Public Instruction Reports and the Census and other records of the Government and other records one could realize these variations.

The reason for the varying trends in the strength of the schools and pupils could not be exactly enumerated. As it will be an elaborate task to find out each and every progress into account, a sort of quinquennial and decadal assessment on the general improvement made in the education of the Muslims is considered.

As according to the Administrative Records of Madras Presidency of 1900-1901 and the report of the Director of Public Instruction of 1901 the following state of condition was recorded in the progress of education of the Muslims. There was a satisfactory advance in the number and strength in Muslim institutions, the figures for the year under report being highest for the last 5 years. The number of public institutions was 1054, and their strength was 47,368, the number of private institutions was 1076 with strength of 32,968.[14]

The number of male students in the collegiate stage of instruction was 80 in Arts College and 7 in Professional colleges. In the secondary stage the numbers were 558 in the Upper secondary and 1766 in the Lower secondary; while in the primary stage also the number rose to 58,369. There were no girls above the lower secondary stage and the number in this stage was 29, in the primary stage there were 10,912 girls. In Training Schools, there were 67 male students and 10 females, and in other special schools 341 and 34 respectively. On the whole there were 60,773 boys and 10,941 girls receiving a general education and 415 boys and 44 girls in special Schools.[15]

Primary School Education

The number of Public Primary schools for Mohammedans was 1,037 and their strength was 45,915. There was an increase of 177 schools and 9,246 pupils of the primary schools 45.8 per cent were managed in the previous year. The number of boys appeared for the primary examination was 1,563, of whom 918 passed against 857 out of 1516 in 1900-01.[16] These results showed a fair improvement.

Secondary Education

The number of secondary schools for Mohammedans was 10; two of these were Upper secondary schools with a total strength of 450, lower secondary. Schools for Mohammedans increased in number by one and in strength by 26. At the Matriculation and Lower secondary examinations 195 and 371 respectively appeared and 50 and 74 passed, while in 1900-01 26 and 81 passed out of 182 and 412. There was a marked increase in the number that passed the Matriculation results at the last examination. For the Upper secondary examination 7 appeared and 2 passed in 1901-02 and one passed out of four in 1900-1901.

In Upper secondary examinations, there appeared 128 male and 3 female students; of them 98 were Brahmins and 29 non-Brahmin caste Hindus. Among the 4 Mohammedan students appeared only 1 passed. In Matriculation examinations 7313 appeared, out of them only 1423 passed. Among the passed there were 44 Europeans, 133 native Christians, 29 Mohammedans, 932 Brahmins and 285 non-Brahmin Hindus.[17]

Collegiate Education

In Collegiate education in Arts Colleges, 23 students attended the Madras Christian College and 18 students attended the Presidency College. Of the 24 candidates who appeared for one or more parts of the B.A, degree examination, only 7 qualified for the degree. In the FA examinations, out of 35 appeared only 11 passed in Arts and 15 passed in Science. On the whole there showed a fair improvement except in Science which was 46 in the previous year.[18] The Caste wise and religion wise exact figures were not available.

Special Education

Special schools for Mohammedans fell in number from 8 to 7 and in strength from 262 to 254 during the year 1900-01. The decrease was due to the closing of the Industrial school at Asur, Cuddapah, known as Dabistani Kauphia Bagini seminary. The Law College and the College for Agriculture had each two Mohammedan students and there was one each in the Medical and Engineering colleges. There were 10 Mohammedan pupils attending the school of Arts, 39 attending the school of Medicine and 2 attending the school of Engineering. Of the 35 Mohammedan male students under training, 20 belonged to the Mohammedan branch Training School in Madras, 15 to the Mappillah Training School in Malapuram. Of the female students under training 6 were in the Government Hobart Training School, Madras and two in the school at Gunnairbeed. The two Industrial schools specially intended for Mohammedans, viz, the Anjuman-i-Mufidi Ahle Islam in Madras and the one for Mohammedan women at Guntur had respectively 100 and 31 pupils on their rolls.[19]

Scholarships

The Government has extended scholarships to 42 Mohammedan students, which include 18 Lower secondary, 13 Upper secondary, 9 F.A and 2 B.A. The total expenditure for Muslim education was Rs. 2,67,127. Of the special school for Mohammedans there were 8 with 262 pupils against

6 with 202 pupils last year, the increase was due to the opening of industrial classes in connection with 2 Mohammedan schools one at Cuddapah and the other at Vellore.

The number of Muslim students in the College of Agriculture was 2, Engineering College 1, Law College 2 and Medical College 2. Only 20 pupils attended school of Arts and 35 the Madras school of Medicine. In the Training school there were 109 pupils of whom 26 were Mappillahs, while 6 female students under training, 3 were at Hobart Training School, Madras and 3 in Gunairbeed.[20]

The Collegiate Education, in March 1901, 532 candidates were admitted to degrees against 511 in the previous year. In M.A degree 36 appeared and 19 passed. In B.A degree 856 appeared (including 4 girls) 354 passed. Among 1,198 B.A degree candidates, Tanjore contributed as usually the largest number 233 and Malabar coming next with 83 students. A scholarship of Rs. 20 per annum was awarded to 4 M.A. Degree graduates and 8 scholarships of Rs. 10 per annum to B.A degree graduates (3 scholarships to Backward Classes, 1 to Uriyas and remaining 4 to Mohammedans). Moreover 25 FA scholarships of Rs 7 (7 to girls – 6 to Brahmins – 6 to Mohammedans 4 to Backward Classes – 2 to Uriyas) The Fees collected was Rs. 85.0 and 71-13 respectively while it was 79.10 and 73-14 last year.[21]

Judged by the statistics, the education of Mohammedans may be considered to have made progress during the year 1911. The number of institutions specially intended for them rose from 2,049 to 2,147 and their strength from 87,025 to 97287, the increase being shared both by public and private institutions. Unaided institutions, however, presented a decrease in both respects due to the transfer of some of them to the aided list. The opening of the Government Mohammedans girl's school, Mylapore, raised the number of Government schools from 55 to 56. The total number of Mohammedans under instruction in all classes and grades of schools rose from 1,28,835 including 24,867 girls, to 1,36,428 including 26,317 girls. The percentage to the total

Mohammedan population of school age was being 37 against 34.9 in the previous year. But there was a fall in the Mohammedans strength from 84 to 69 in Arts Colleges. In Matric, 154 appeared 20 passed. However in subsequent years there was an increase in the percentage of the total number of Mohammedan scholars in all classes of institutions to the Mohammedan population of school age from 37.4 to 39.6.[22]

The policy of offering special inducements to the Muslim community as mentioned in the last quinquennium i.e. 1901-05 report continued in force, though the changes made in 1906 in the Educational and Grant-in Aid rules altered the form of some of them.[23] In all institution of all grades under Public Management, a Mohammedan student need only to pay fees at half the rate charged in the case of other students. The institutions under Private Management almost invariably granted the same concession, and in nearly all branches of education above the elementary grade, scholarships are either reserved for Mohammedans or they have a preference. In the case of Mappillah, an especially backward class of Mohammedans, scholarships tenable in elementary schools were also awarded. Mohammedan students under training as teachers received a higher rate of stipend. Nearly one half of the total number of public funds and over 70 per cent of the rest were aided.[24]

It was disappointing to find that these efforts on the part of the Government have so far evoked so little effective response from the Muslims and that there has been so little progress in the education especially the higher education of Mohammedans. There has, however been some progress, in the higher education of the quinquennium. The signs were improving in one or two of the central and southern districts where a demand for secondary education was beginning to make itself felt, and the member of the community have come forward with proposals for establishing and endowing high schools.

Mohammedans Scholars Under Instruction

One hundred and nineteen thousand Mohammedans were returned as being under instruction on March 31st, 1907.[25] This number included 39,000 pupils attending private institution for Mohammedans, which were almost entirely Quran schools and in which little or no secular instruction is given and 3,000 in other private institution, mostly indigenous elementary schools. The remaining 77,000 were attending public institutions.[26]

The pupils' strength in public institutions for Mohammedans was 49,000 and excluding the small number of Hindus and native Christians to be found in Mohammedans schools, the number of Mohammedans reading in Mohammedan public schools might be taken at 48,000 leaving about 29,000 Mohammedans in attendance in non-Mohammedan public schools. The above figures in each case represent an advance on those for 1901-1902, but the increase is small and practically was made in the last year of the quinquennium except In the case of the Quran schools, the Mohammedans in public schools were in the primary stage, less than one percent were reading in high school classes.[27] The request of Mohammedan people of Mangalore to establish an Anglo-Hindustani School was rejected by the Government and they were informed that enough has been already done.[28]

Primary Education

The number and strength of Mohammedans primary schools fell during the first four years of the quinquennium (1901-1905), but there was a recovery in 1906-1907 and their total strength at the end of the period stood higher than at the beginning. Taking into account Mohammedan pupil in other primary schools there has been an increase of 6.5 per cent. The number of Mohammedan pupils increased in primary schools, most of which occurred in the last year of the quinquennium.[29]

Secondary Education

There were only two high schools for Mohammedans, the Government Madrasa-I-Azam and the Harris high school, managed by the Church Missionary Society, both situated in Madras. The former was provided in 1903-1904 with commodious building with spacious playing grounds and a hostel for the accommodation of students coming from the rural areas. The efficiency of the institution had improved in 1906-07. The number of Mohammedan boys in high school classes had increased by 22 per cent in the quinquennium.[30]

Collegiate Education

The number of Mohammedans reading in Arts colleges had been small throughout the period and had varied irregularly, being lowest in 1906-07. The number in professional colleges had fluctuated still more irregularly and at the period there were only 15 Mohammedan students preparing for the liberal professions, two for law, one for medicine. The number of Mohammedans who proceeded to the University in spite of the facilities offered to them is very disappointing.[31]

Female Education

Of the 22,000 Mohammedan girls receiving instruction as on March 31st, 1907, 10,000 were reading in Quran schools, and 12,000 in public institutions. The later were almost entirely in the primary stage of instruction; of them nearly 5,000 were attending public schools for Mohammedan girls, and the remainder in other public schools.

There had been an increase in the number of Mohammedan girls attending public as well as private institutions amounting in the case of the former to nearly 17 per cent. The increase in the case of Public institutions occurred mainly in the last year of quinquennium. The Government was maintaining 35 schools for Mohammedan girls with strength of about 1,600. The Mohammedans girls who proceeded beyond the fourth standard were numbered in tens, it stood at 29 at the beginning of the period and 57 at the end.[32]

Special Education

The special schools intended for Mohammedans comprise three training schools, two for masters and one for mistresses and in the three industrial schools, two for boys and one a school of embroidery for girls. The most important of the industrial schools is the Anjuman-Mufid-I-Ahle-Islam in Madras which usually had 100 boys on the rolls, and to which the Government had given an annual grant of Rs. 5,000 for several years.

The number of Mohammedans, especially the girls, under training as teachers, was regrettably small during the period and it was always a matter of difficult to fill up appointments in the Mohammedan schools with qualified teachers. It is also a matter of regret that the number of Mohammedans in schools decreased from 41 to 22 in this period.[33]

Cookery Classes for Teachers

With a view to improve the teaching of domestic economy, arrangements were made in February 1912, with a course of lectures and demonstration in cookery to teachers in European schools in Madras. In this connection a lady lecturer was appointed, who was for nine and-a-half years served as a Domestic Economy and a Hygiene Instructress under the London country council. Added to that, she subsequently had experience of household management in the Presidency. It was anticipated that it would later be found practicable to organize similar courses with an extended range of subjects.[34]

Progress of Mohammedan Education

In the Report of the Director of Public Instruction of the Madras Presidency of 1911-12, in the quinquennial report it had to deplore the comparative failure of the efforts made by the Government for the extension of Mohammedan education to evoke response from the community, but it was also mentioned that in the last year of the quinquennium there were not wanting indications that the community's indifference to education was breaking down and that more rapid progress might be anticipated in the future. This anticipation had been realized so far as increase in numbers under instruction goes. In the quinquennium from 1902-03 to 1906-07 the total increase was only 8 percent., whereas in the years to which this report refers the increase had been nearly 23 per cent. That is, the rate of increase had been three times as rapid. This increase had however been almost confined to the lower stages of instruction. The number in the Arts College rose from 76 in 1906-07 to 96 in 1911-12, the number in professional college has slightly fallen and the number in secondary schools after some fluctuations had returned to very nearly what it was at the beginning of the quinquennium.[35]

Apathy and intellectual indolence and the postponement of secular to religious instruction on doubt went for to account for these facts. The community moreover was poor and some families who were otherwise keeping their boys at schools were not able to find the money for fees. It was also both a cause and consequence of indifference to higher education that well-to-do Mohammedans were so commonly in business and perhaps this indicated a prevalence of common sense. The number of secondary schools in which Urdu was the medium of instruction, still very small and in other schools Mohammedans were at a disadvantage in the lower classes where a Dravidian language was the medium of instruction.[36] These causes account for the absence of progress in secondary education and while this remained stationary, the fluctuations in the numbers in college may be regarded as merely accidental.

The number of schools had increased by 110. Seven Government elementary schools all for girls had been added and brought the total of Government schools up to 60. Local and Municipal boards had also increased the number of their schools. There were 450 such schools in 1907-08 and 520 at the end of the quinquennium. The number of aided schools rose by 140, while that of unaided private schools had somewhat diminished. The increase in schools had been most marked in Public schools intended for Mohammedans, amounting to 33 per cent., while in Public institutions generally it was 27 per cent. This comparatively small difference was very far from indicating the degree of preference for their own schools on the part of Mohammedans, because most parents could not exercise any choice in the matter, the only accessible school being one not specially intended for them. There had been an increase of over 1,000 in the number of pupils in private schools.[37]

There were a number of private Quran schools run by private people not complied with departmental requirements and imparting little secular instruction were also admitted to receive grant from the government. These schools were almost confined to two or three southern districts where Labbais, Marakaiyars and backward classes of Mohammedans were numerous. Attempts had been made, with some success, to induce the teachers in these schools to add secular instruction to their religious instruction, which constituted of learning Arabic scriptures which were understood by neither the pupil nor the teacher, had no much value except mental discipline.[38]

After a decade, judged by the statistics, the education of the Mohammedans had made further progress (i.e. between 1901 and 1910). The number of institutions specially intended for them rose to 2291. The strength of the Mohammedan students in elementary schools was 95,767. The number of students in collegiate education in B.A., level was 69. Public schools were 1149. However there was a decrease in the number of Private schools. Unaided institutions, however presented a decrease in both respects due to the transfer of some of them to the aided list. There was increase in the Mohammedan girls' strength. The opening of the Government Mohammedan girls' school, Mylapore, raised the number of Government schools from 55 to 56. The total number of Mohammedans under the instruction in all classes and grades of schools rose from 1,28,835 including 24,867 girls to 1,36,428 including 26,317 girls, the percentage to the total Mohammedan population of school age being 37 against 34.9

in the previous year. But there was a fall in the Mohammedans strength from 84 to 69 in Arts Colleges. In Matriculation, 154 appeared and 20 passed. The total expenditure on Mohammedan education during the year 1910-11 was Rs.3, 95, 147.[39] The increase was mainly due to the opening of 218 schools for the benefit of this community by local Boards and Municipal councils out of the additional funds placed by Government at their disposal. Five sectional schools were at work during the year, which accounts for the increase from 86 to 203 in the strength of the Training Schools intended for Mohammedans.[40]

There was an advance also in the number of Mohammedan schools, Arts Colleges and Secondary schools for non-Europeans, the numbers having risen from 96 and 5507 to 125 and 5885, respectively. Consistently with the advance indicated by the facts mentioned above the percentage of the total number of Mohammedan schools in all classes of institutions to the Mohammedan population of school age rose from 35.5 to 37.4. Of the public schools intended for Mohammedans 135 were elementary schools for girls attended by 7,260 pupils, these figures showing an advance of four in the number of schools and about 500 in their strength. The total number of private institutions and their strength showed a decline during the year; but this is not altogether a matter for regret, as it was in part due to the classification as public schools of such of the private institutions as confirmed to the departmental standards of instruction.[41]

The increase during the year in the total number of Mohammedan pupils under instruction in all classes and grades of institutions may be taken as evidence of the increasing educational activity of the Muslim community not with standing the fall in the number of schools specially intended for them, this fall was however confined to private schools, which were generally of an ephemeral character. The condition of education in the Laccadive Muslims continued to be satisfactory according to the report furnished by the Collector of Malabar.

Generally the field of education suffered without progress because of the First World War. Due to this Great War the British Government of India diverted its attention and its exchequer to meet the needs of the war and there was little progress made in the education of the Muslims also. Another setback occurred in the progress of education of the Muslims, was the Khilafat Movement. During this movement the Muslim students came out of the Colleges and Schools to revolt against the British Government of India. Moreover, Gandhiji gave a call for boycotting English schools and foreign articles. The Muslims immediately responded to it and boycotted the British institutions. Due to this reason there was a great fall in the strength of the students in almost all the levels of education. This decrease was mainly in elementary schools because the Muslim parents boycotted the British schools and opened several unrecognized schools under private management. So the strength of the Mohammedan institutions intended for them fell to 1983. In arts colleges there were only 138 Mohammedan students, which was 24 less than the previous year. However, Mohammedan students in secondary schools for Indians rose to 8210 that was an increase by 237. The elementary schools' strength fell to 1,14,014, which was a decrease by 4420 than the previous year. The total expenditure was Rs. 11, 48,000.[42]

The growing discontentment on the suppressive policy of the British Government steadily kindled among the Muslims a desire for western education. It created an urge among them to found new independent educational institutions. In order to remove the official control on education as introduced by Lord Curzon a resolution was passed in the Legislature in the year 1913. But this could not be given effect due to the First World War calamity. After the Great War the education of the Muslims was further affected by the Khilafat movement of 1919. But in spite of these hurdles an epoch making attempt was made for first time in the history of South India. In Madras Presidency at Vaniyambadi of North Arcot District, the 'Islamiah College' was founded under the philanthropic munificence of the Muslims.

Efforts of Vaniyambadi Muslim Educational Society

Islamiah College is a symbol of devotion to education and love for learning of the Muslims of Vaniyambadi who in their zeal for translating into action the message of Sir Syed Ahamed khan established the Vaniyambadi Muslim Educational Society in 1901.The society was registered in 1905 and soon under its auspices the Islamic Elementary School was started. The phenomenal growth of the school was due to the untiring and dedicated service and leadership of Hajee T. Badruddin Sahib, Malang Hayath Batcha Sahib, T.Ameenuddin Sahib and Malang Ahamed Batcha Sahib. The full-fledged Islamiah High school came into being in 1912.[43]

In 1915, the Vaniyambadi educational Society resolved to establish the Islamiah College and the foundation stone of the College was laid by His Excellency Lord Pentland, the then Governor of Madras Province. With princely donations from the Muslim philanthropists, the College was started in 1919 and got recognition from July 1921. The building in the College is housed at present was opened by Nawab C.Abdul Hakeem Sahib who gave a munificent donation of Rs. 50,000 to the society.

The College keeps its portals open to the members of all castes and communities. From its very inception it has drawn members on its establishment, staff and students from all communities. The aim of the college is to foster the teachers and students, and through them the society in general, the attitudes and values needed for developing 'good life' in individuals and in the society.

The Director of Public Instruction Records and Administrative Report of Madras Presidency were not having sufficient information about the progress made during the First World War and Khilafat Movement. The only information available was that the Government had raised the Madarasa-I-Azam to the status of second Grade College, the junior and senior intermediate classes being opened in it during this period. The Strength was 19 (i.e. 10 Junior and 9 senior) on the 13th March 1919.[44]

Dyarchy was introduced by the British Government in 1919. Subsequently, the Justice party won in the election in the year 1920 and formed the Ministry. The Justice party Government formed in the Madras Presidency fought for more power for the Provincial Governments and as a result of this education was transferred as a State subject in 1921. This transfer of Education Department to the State helped a lot to develop the education of the local people especially of the women. But the growth of education of the Muslims still remained under an unappreciable state. The Muslims of south were still under a state of confusion and dilemma. Even in the Hindu society the progress of education was highly advanced in the Brahmin community where as other caste Hindus' advancement was not up to the expectation. Next to Brahmins the Christians were far advanced than the Muslims especially in women's education. The steady expansion of western education did not reach fully to the Muslims of the Madras Presidency, unlike that of their counter parts in North India.

The Government Mohammedan College at Madras was continued for a further term of one year on a temporary basis. The Islamiah College Vaniyambadi, whose very existence was seriously threatened in the previous two years by the Khilafat and Non-Cooperation Movements, regained its stability. There was a very satisfactory increase from 141 to 184 in the number of students in Arts colleges. The number of Professional colleges increased slightly from 41 to 44.[45]

The Government Mohammedan College of Madras is still located in Madarasa-I-Azam compound building. The lack of accommodation hurdled further improvement of the college, further more to view, some of the students of the Mohammedan College have to attend some classes at Presidency College. To take up Urdu in the Intermediate classes, the Mohammedan students of Presidency College have to attend the Mohammedan College.[46]

The Church Missionary Society decided to discontinue the Harris High school, Royapattah, from 23rd June 1923, the Government sanctioned taking over of the management of the school by the department temporarily to the end of April 1924 with a view to enabling the Mohammedan community in the mean while to arrange for the conduct of the school as an aided institution. Towards the cost of maintenance of the school by the Department, the Mohammedan Educational Association of Southern India contributed a sum of RS. 3000.[47]

The Government noticed with special satisfaction the progress that had been made in the education of Mohammedans and the depressed classes. There was a very large increase in the number of Mohammedans attending all classes of instructions.[48]

The Government had realized that the General policy on mass education needed some urgent reforms. It decided to eliminate inefficient and ineffective schools and to establish in their places well equipped, complete five standard schools so that the people enrolled in them might go through the full primary course and become permanently literate. Various measures were adopted to achieve this object. The Government was glad to note that they have begun to produce satisfactory results.

At the close of the year 1930, the Madras Administrative Report reveals the condition of the education of the Muslims as follows... the total number of institutions intended for Muslims rose from 3692 to 3902. The pupils' strength increased from 2, 17,262 to 2, 26,449. But the number of private institutions decreased from 650 to 572. Their strength also fell from 27,969 to 25,261. The secondary schools intended for Mohammedans increased to 3768. Thus, during this year 17 secondary schools for boys and 1 for girls was started. In Secondary schools for Indians the Mohammedan strength also increased from 10,710 to 11,376. The total expenditure during this year was Rs.22,97,000.[49]

The Mohammedan population of the Madras Presidency increased from 2,840,488 in 1921 to 3,305,937. In 1931, there were 3,13,810 men and 29,718 women literates among the Mohammedans. Total ratio of the population, 19.2 per cent of men 1.8 per cent of women were literate. Among others i.e. Hindus 15.6 per cent men and 2.2 per cent women were literates. It is to be noticed that literacy was more advanced among Mohammedan men than their counter parts in Hindu community.[50] The literacy among the Mohammedan women was less advanced.

The Administrative Report of Madras Presidency of 1931-32 shows an overall decrease in the number of Primary Muslim institutions specially intended for them from 3913 to 3110. But the strength of students increased from 2,31,768 to 2,35,439. The Private institutions where also decreased from 579 to 505 and students strength from 24,035 to 20,803. In the Secondary schools the strength of the Muslim students rose from 11,905 to 12,063 whereas in the Secondary schools specially intended for the Muslims the strength of the Muslim students decreased from 3,808 to 3,616. The Muslim students consist of 6 per cent of the overall total strength of the Secondary schools. Total expenditure on Muslim education went from 24.78 lakhs to 27.90 lakhs.[51] One could see these sorts of variations and contradictions in the number of institutions and strength of the students often occurring in the education of the Muslims.

Public Schools especially intended for Mohammedans further decreased from 3487 to 3391 but the strength increased from 2,84,870 to 2,89,387. The Private Schools' strength slightly increased from 225 to 235 and the pupils' strength rose from 8738 to 9249. The number of Secondary schools decreased from 17 to 16 and the strength also decreased from 4093 to 3748. This sort of ups and downs often happened in the education of the Muslims. But to our surprise one more secondary school for girls was added and the strength increased from 421 to 502. In the field of higher education, in Arts Colleges the strength increased from 579 to 685. There were 139 Mohammedan students in Government Arts College, Madras, 35 in Islamiah College, Vaniyambadi. To be precise, the over all strength of students in all secondary Schools increased to 14,657. In that there were 13,631 boys and 1,026 girls. The total expenditure on education was 30.81 lakhs.[52]

A general retrenchment introduced in the public expenditure in the year 1932-33 was reconsidered and possible relaxations to some extent were introduced in the educational expenditure in 1933-34. A cut in the teaching grants imposed was restored. Embargo on new schemes for the provisions of building and equipment for educational institutions were removed.[53] This gave an opportunity to the Muslim people to improve their educational institutions.

The list of backward classes appended to the Madras education rules was revised in the year 1935 by the government. Religious instructors post were sanctioned for two years to the government Mohammedan college of Madras, the government Mohammedan secondary school, Madras and Teacher training school, Madras. [54] The Muslims were very much happy over the above measure taken by the government to impart moral and religious instructions to the students in the school level and colleges.

The quinquennial report on the administration of the Madras Presidency, 1935-36 shows a slight increase in the number of Public institutions of the Muslims from 3601 to 3617 and the pupils' strength also rose from 2,48,905 to 2,60,272. There was also a slight increase in the number of Private institutions of the Muslims from 520 to 523 but their pupils' strength fell from 20,362 to 20,115. The number of secondary schools specially intended for the Muslims remains unchanged (16 schools for boys and 1 school for girls) but their strength rose from 3655 to 3750. The Muslim students' strength studying in secondary schools for Indians increased from 11,943 to 12,465. The number of Muslim students in the Arts colleges, which fell to 466 in the previous year, now rose to 504. The total expenditure on the education of Muslims slightly decreased from 27.06 lakhs to 26.43 lakhs.[55]

The Director of Public Instructions of 1937-38 gives information on the general policy introduced by the Government to eliminate inefficient and ineffective educational institutions in the promotion of mass education. Well equipped complete and standard schools were encouraged with special grants, so that the pupils enrolled in them might go through the full course and became permanently literate. Various measures had been adapted to achieve this object. The government was glad to note that these have been begun to produce satisfactory results among the Muslims. Because of the above said policy, the number of Public schools intended for Mohammedans decreased as also their strength. The number of Private schools also decreased. In colleges also the strength of the Muslims fell from 554 to 549.[56] This condition was changed in the very next year.

The Director of Public Instructions report of 1939-40 shows that though the Public schools intended for Mohammedans decreased from 3,487 to 3,391 the students' strength increased from 2,84,870 to 2,89,387. The number of Private schools increased from 225 to 235 and the pupils' strength rose from 8,738 to 9,249. There was a great increase in the number of Muslim students in Arts Colleges; it rose from 579 to 685. The Government had started one more Secondary school for the Muslim girls. The overall strength of the Muslim students studying in Secondary schools increased from 14,387 to 14,657 among that 1,026 were girls. The total expenditure of the Muslim education increased from 30.48 lakhs to 31.81 lakhs.[57]

The period between 1938 and 1945 hampered the interest of the British Government in Indian Administration due to Second World War. Like that of the Great War period there was stagnation in the implementation of reforms and developments all over India. So, the progress of the Education of the Muslims was not given more attention. The Madras Administrative Report and the Director of Public Instruction records have little information about the improvement of the education of the Muslims during this period.

State Government Scholarship

Anyhow, the Administrative report of the Government of Madras Presidency of 1945 refers to the residential scholarships offered by the Government to the unmarried Hindu and Muslim girls. Six scholarships with a monthly value of Rs.18 each were awarded for 10 months in a year to unmarried Hindu girls and 2 scholarships to the same value to unmarried Muslim girls studying in recognized schools having recognized hostel.[58] These scholarships were tenable in standards IX to XI of secondary schools each year. Scholarships were awarded to Hindu and Muslim widows in standards IV to XI of Secondary schools. Every year 21 scholarships with a monthly value of RS 8 for 10 months in a year were awarded to the girl students in general.[59]

The Administrative report of the Madras Presidency, 1945-46 reveals the condition of the education of the Muslims as follow: the number of Secondary schools intended for Muslims were 22 for boys and 11 for girls. There were 6,396 boys and 1,837 girls studying in these schools. The total number of Muslim students all over the secondary schools was 24,378, among that 22,163 were boys and 2,125 were girls. There were 190 scholars studying in the Arabic Colleges established by the Muslims. The strength of Muslim students in the Arts Colleges was 1,233 and in Professional Colleges it was 213. The total expenditure on the education of the Muslims was 58.11 lakhs.[60]

A Comparative Study on the Three Religious Groups

A comparative study on the three religious groups derived from the census records show the educational condition of the Muslim population before Independence. Educationally the Brahmins are the leaders of Southern India. In view of what "education" at present represents, it was permissible to consider whether the Brahmins' pre- eminence was altogether to their unmixed advantage. For example, in comparison a Brahmin as a meteorologist whereas a non-Brahmin a carpenter.[61]

"The intellectual endowment of each and every Brahmin is sufficient for acquiring the literary education that will serve him as a sufficient pecuniary stay of life. Yet to great extent the Brahmin whose traditional priesthood is scarcely now a practical calling has cut himself off form all professions, save those who practice demands some tincture of literacy; with a consequent result that he has over stocked his own market. And it is curious to notice how in this clerical market Indian opinion tends to regulate advancement by the passing of literary examinations to the disregard of practical ability; and thus to forge chains for its own community."[62]

Among Mohammedans, the Labbais, as one would expect from the addiction to trade, far outstrip their co-religionist in the literacy of their men; although they are below the general Mohammedan level in female literacy and the literacy in English.[63]

Christian education, deduction of the European and Anglo-Indian communities affects considerably the figures elsewhere quoted. But, considering the social class from which the Indian Christian community is largely recruited, their educational position and progress can hardly be deemed as other than creditable.[64]

Among the Muslim population other than the Urdu speaking Muslims most of them were converted to Islam from the various castes of Hinduism especially from the backward classes and suppressed people. So, the educational development of the Muslims should be placed on par with them only. Hence, the concession demanded by the Muslims and extended by the British Government is justified.

The apparent raise in the literacy of Mohammedans and to a less extent Christians reflects their small figures in total. On the other hand, Mohammedans largely, in general, are traders and consequently would tend to be more literate than their co-religionist elsewhere. The general higher literacy rate of Mohammedan males than Hindus in the Circars and East Coast Central and South (Thanjavur and Trichinopoly comes under South East Coast) to some extent reflect their differing positions. An essentially trading community will always tend to have greater literacy. Mohammedan figures for the west coast bear this out, for there they are much less literate and there they are a cultivating as distinct from a primarily trading class.[65]

Gender	Hindus			Muslims			Christians		
	S	E	C	S	W	C	S	W	C
Males	16	5	2	19	5	2	6	3	2
Females	22	6	1	18	4	1	12	7	5

S, W, C represents South, West and Central respectively in East Coast region.

The great superiority of Christians in English literacy already commented on is apparent in their acquisition of the fifth standard stage and once again is largely a feature of West Coast. The Hindu attainment of continuing literacy is at its strongest in the East Coast South and Mohammedan in the East Coast South and Central. For females the ratios are Hindus-22:6:1, Muslims-18:4:1 and Christians 12:7:5.[66]

Here the East Coast Central leads with Christians. The disturbing influence of Madras city is apparent in all literacy considerations affecting this division and its presence tends to give the division a higher literacy record than is really its due. The two-ratio sequence approximated much more closely for Christians than for the other two communities, another indication of the greater leveling up of sex education among them.[67]

The title 'Education' has been altered to 'Literacy' from the 1931 Census records. The change is to be appreciable because Literacy is not Education but merely a means to that end and while figures can show with some degree of accuracy how the first is advancing, much more than statistics of quantity is required to assess the progress of education. If this has to be taken in its broadest meaning of knowledge and understanding of life and of men, the literacy key is not even indispensable although useful and desirable. "The key metaphor is probably the best; all that literacy can do is open a door; the use made of the access is another and much difficult matter, one on which in India as in Europe there has been much questioning."[68]

During 1931-32 a number of G.Os had been issued for the development of the education of the Muslims. The native Newspapers particularly the Muslim Newspapers invited the attention of the Government on the problems connected with the education of the Muslims. They published the matter or the complaints of the people and appealed to the Government. Generally, the Government also took a sympathetic attitude towards the subject. The grievances were often heard and solved. Such Newspapers, which rendered services to the cause of the education of the Muslims, are the following: Shamsul-Akhbar - Triplicane, Jam Bazaar, Madras, Mazhar-ul- Ajaib - Triplicane, Jam Bazaar, Madras, Tilism-i-Hairat - Triplicane, Jam Bazaar, Madras Jaridahi Rozgar - Triplicane, Royappetah, Madras, Jalva-i-Sakhun - Triplicane, Madras, Muslim Mitran – Madras, Qaumi Report – Vaniyambadi and The Muhammadan - Madras.

Apart from these, there were Muslim Newspapers also from Bangalore and Hyderabad, which threw light on the local problems of the education of the Muslims. The All India Muslim Educational Conference, which held in Madras in December 1901, requested the Government to give much attention and priority to the development of the mass education of the Muslims.[69]

The Anjuman-i-Mufidi Ahle Islam, an association, had furnished certain G.Os relating to the employment of Musalmans in the Public services.[70] This sort of service enabled the Muslims to apply for such jobs. The request of the inhabitants of Mangalore to establish Anglo-Hindustani schools in their localities was published in the Newspaper 'The Mohammadan' which reached the Government. But the Government refused the appeal and said that enough had already been done.[71]

A Board of Muhammadan Education formed in 1900 was recognized by the Government and it had been supplied with copies of Government Orders related to the education of the Muslims.[72] We could find a number of G.Os issued by the Law and Education Department of the Government which gives information about the salary of the teachers, building grants, sanction of play ground sites, sanction of the scholarships and fee concessions extended to the Muslim students. The Government had passed G.O even for the admission of Non-Muslim girl students in the Government Hobart Training School specially intended for the Muslim girls.[73] This sort of situation arose because of the lack of enrolment of the Muslim girls in the school. In order to fill the vacancies, the Government had to enroll the Non-Muslim girls.

An Urdu Newspaper namely, Qaumi Report declared that illiteracy of India especially of Muhammadans is mainly due to the use in education a difficult foreign language, English! It declared that a language (Hindustani) should be adopted as a common instructional vernacular of India.[74] But the Indian languages in those days were not developed with scientific terms and other necessary things to have as a common instructional language. Now-a-days, the Indian languages have developed to a greater extent; the above said opinion may be tried.

Mr. Zynul Abidin, a political and an educational exponent wrote an article in a Newspaper remarked that it was a pity that the Muhammadan community denied the privileges as enjoyed by the Europeans - a community much smaller than the Muhammadans in the Madras Presidency.[75] This criticism by Mr. Zynul Abidin made the Government to think over it. In another Muslim Newspaper, the want of Technical schools for the Muhammadan community had been pointed out and requested the Government to take necessary steps for the establishment of the Technical schools and factories in Madras.[76]

The Muslims gave much importance to their religion and there was a fear in their mind that their children studying in schools will go out side the fold of Islam. In order to remove this fear psychosis, the Government appointed a committee in 1931, to consider and report on certain problems connected with the education of the Muhammadans. The Committee's report with the remarks of the Director of Public Instruction was submitted to the Government in March 1932. The Committee pointed out that the education of the Muhammadans will not be complete unless the teaching of the Quran and the traditions of the Prophet forms a part the Curriculum... and that to this end religious instruction should be made an integral part of school education.[77] And it further recommended that the expenditure incurred in imparting religious instruction to Muhammadan students should be a legitimate charge on the resources of Government and Local bodies. The religious instructions should be given to Muhammadan pupils within school hours not only in schools, chiefly intended for them but also in other schools under Public management and under the management of the Non-mission aided agencies and that the expenditure incurred on the salaries of religious instructions for Muhammadan pupils in aided schools should be taken into account for the purpose of assessment of grants.

On these recommendations the Government replied that under the existing rules, public funds (including the funds of Local bodies) could not be used for the purpose of imparting religious instructions in schools. It pointed out that the suggestions made by the Committee involve a radical change in the policy hitherto followed by the Government. But the Government decided after careful consideration that the time had come for further relaxation of the policy hitherto pursued in this matter. The Government was accordingly prepared to accept the principles.[78]

Orders had been passed in this matter to all types of schools and the Director of Public instruction was requested to submit proposals for the provision of religious instruction in Government schools intended for Muhammadans, so that they might be considered in connection with part second of the budget estimates for 1934-35.[79]

In response to the repeated demands of the Muhammadan community for a separate college for Muhammadans in Madras, as the Government could not give immediate effect to it, a budget motion was passed in the Legislative Council of the Madras Presidency in 1918. Accordingly Intermediate classes were opened by the Government in Madarasa-i-Azam campus in 1918 and B.A classes were added to it in 1920 and in due course, Science and Mathematic groups were introduced. The College was upgraded as first grade College in 1928, and adequate steps were taken to introduce more courses and keep it efficient as first grade college.[80] Fee concessions to girls, both Mohammedans pupils and to pupils of backward communities were governed by the Madras Educational rules. A condition in the rule quoted above, limited the half fee concessions admissible under it to the poor among girls, pupils of the Muhammadan and the backward communities.

Further representations had been made by the Muslim private bodies and discussions had been raised in the budget sessions to urge the Government that the full fee concessions might be allowed to the Muhammadan pupils irrespective of their poverty. The Director of Public Instruction advised on the question that the condition of poverty should be enforced in every case of educational concession in secondary schools and colleges. The extra cost of removing the poverty status in the case of all pupils affected by rule 92 of the Madras Educational Rules was estimated in 1925 by Director of Public Instruction as 1.33 lakhs. The Government had concurred in the Director of Public Instruction's G.O stated that they do not propose to make any general modification in rule 92 of the Madras Educational Rules.[81] Thus full fee concession under poverty status was not extended to the Muslims. The educated and Nationalist Muslims vehemently criticized this stand of the Government.

In 1922, Rao Bahadur M.C. Raja proposed a resolution in the Legislative Council meeting demanding 15 per cent of seats to the depressed classes and 15 per cent of seats to the Muhammadans to be reserved in the professional colleges of the Madras Presidency.[82] But unfortunately this resolution was not moved in the Council, but the papers were recorded. There was some endowment scholarships instituted by Muslim philanthropists made available to the Muhammadan students in Arts colleges and Professional colleges especially in Medical colleges. They were: The Boddam Muslim Memorial Scholarship Endowment.[83] The Dharmapuri Zamindar Muhammad Khan Sahib Endowment.[84] Muslim Educational Association of South India scholarships. Wenlock Memorial scholarships to the Medical students.[85]

In the Government scholarship Notification issued, provisions were made for the grant of these scholarships to the college students of the Muhammadan community who were most in need of aid and satisfied other conditions be considered first. In the Legislative Council, budget motions were proposed to increase scholarships to the Muhammadan students.

After Independence no separate measures for the development of the Education of the Muslims had been taken. The Administrative Reports, Director of Public Instruction records, Law and educational records and other Government records after 1947 speak nothing separately about the Education of the Muslim community.

The British Government paid more attention to bring the Muslims forward in education as well as in getting Government jobs. The Muslim Community also responded to it, 'A better late than never' attitude was followed by the Muslims which resulted in their educational development. Even though the development started lately but it was far better than their condition some years ago. But after Independence the free Indian Government followed a secular policy not only in their political ideas but in the field of education also. Because of this 'Secularism' no religion or race was given special importance. The welfare measures were implemented on common basis only. But the Government of India as well as the State Governments started to follow a caste based concessions in education as well as in Government jobs. The suppressed classes of the people under caste system are given priority for rejuvenation and development in the field of education and employment. Thus the Muslims were not considered as suppressed people according to the Government policy. In this juncture, the Muslims realized the gravity of the situation and came forward to start educational institutions of their own for the welfare of their community.

REFERENCES

1. J.A. Richy, *Progress of Education in India*, 1917-22, Vol. I, p. 86.
2. *Ibid.*
3. *Census of India 1901*, Vol. I, Tamil Nadu Archives (T.N.A).
4. *Report of the Mohammedans Educational Endowments Committee* printed by Secretariat Press, Calcutta dated 28th February 1888, National Archives of India, New Delhi.
5. *Report on the Administration of Madras Presidency*, 1900-01, p. 121, T.N.A.
6. *Ibid.*, p. 121.
7. *Ibid.*, p. 121.
8. *Ibid.*, p. 122.
9. *Ibid.*, p. 123.
10. *Census of India 1891*-Madras, Vol-XIII, p.176, T.N.A.
11. *Ibid.*
12. *G.O No. 99, Grant in Aid Sanction*, 5th March 1903, T.N.A.
13. *The All India Muslim Education Conference*, Law and Education Department. Letter to the Secretary dated 29th August 1927, T.N.A.
14. *Report on Public Instruction of the Madras Presidency*, 1901-02, p. 258, T.N.A.

15. *Report on the Public Instruction of the Madras Presidency*, 1900-01, p. 36, T.N.A.
16. *Ibid.*, p. 36.
17. *Ibid.*, p. 37.
18. *Ibid.*, p. 37.
19. *Ibid.*, p. 38.
20. *Ibid.*, p. 38.
21. *Ibid.*, p. 39.
22. *Report of the Director of Public Instruction*, 1910-11, p. 6, T.N.A.
23. *Report of the Director of Public Instruction*, 1913-14, p. 12, T.N.A.
24. *Administrative Report of the Madras Presidency*, 1907-08, p. 94, T.N.A.
25. *Ibid.*
26. *Ibid*, p. 95.
27. *Report on Public Instruction*, Madras Presidency, 1906-07, p.52, T.N.A.
28. *G.O No. 552, Law & Education Dept.* dated 30th September 1901, T.N.A
29. *Report on Public Instruction*, Madras Presidency, 1906-07, p. 52, T.N.A.
30. *Ibid.*, p. 53.
31. *Ibid.*, p. 52.
32. *Ibid.*, p. 52.
33. *Ibid.*, p. 53.
34. *Ibid.*, p.54.
35. *Ibid.*, p.55.
36. *Report on the Public Instruction of Madras Presidency*, 1911-12, p. 55, T.N.A.
37. *Ibid.*
38. *Ibid.*
39. *Ibid.*, p. 56.
40. *Administrative Report of Madras Presidency*, 1911-1912, p. 235, T.N.A.

41. *Administrative Report of Madras Presidency*, 1912-13, p.88, T.N.A.
42. *Ibid.*, p.89.
43. *Administrative Report of Madras Presidency*, 1920-21, p.101, T.N.A.
44. *Account derived from the Magazines and Souvenirs of Islamiah College*, Vaniyambadi, T.N.A.
45. *Report on the Public Instruction of Madras Presidency*, 13th March 1919, p. 11, T.N.A.
46. *Report on the Public Instruction of Madras Presidency*, 1922-23, p. 63, T.N.A.
47. *Report on the Public Instruction of Madras Presidency*, 1923-24, p. 36, T.N.A.
48. *G.O No.142, Law and Education Department*, dated 26th January 1928, T.N.A.
49. *Administrative Report of Madras Presidency*, 1929-30, p. 208, T.N.A.
50. *Census of India 1931*, Madras, Vol-XIV, Part II, T.N.A.
51. *Administrative Record of Madras Presidency*, 1931-32, p. 180, T.N.A.
52. *Report on the Public Instruction of Madras Presidency*, 1932-33, p.30, T.N.A.
53. *Report on the Public Instruction of Madras Presidency*, 1933-34, p.167, T.N.A.
54. *Administrative Report of Madras Presidency*, 1935-36, p. 187, T.N.A.
55. *Ibid.*
56. *Report on the Public Instruction of Madras Presidency*, 1937-38, p. 28, T.N.A.
57. *Report on the Public Instruction of Madras Presidency*, 1939-40, p. 34-35, T.N.A.
58. *Administrative Report of Madras Presidency*, 1944-45, p. 201, T.N.A.
59. *Ibid*, p.202.
60. *Administrative Report of Madras Presidency*, 1945-46, p. 96, T.N.A.
61. *Administrative Report of Madras Presidency*, 1944-45, p. 202, T.N.A.

62. *Census of India 1911*, Madras, Vol. XII, p. 124, T.N.A.
63. *Ibid.*, p. 125.
64. *Ibid.*, p. 126.
65. *Ibid.*, p. 126.
66. *Census of India 1931*, Madras, p. 264, Part I, T.N.A.
67. *Ibid*, Part I, p. 274.
68. *Ibid*, Part I, p. 274.
69. *Administrative Report of Madras Presidency*, 1901, p. 126, T.N.A.
70. *No. 307, Law and Education Department* (Press), dated 2nd May 1901, T.N.A.
71. *No. 552, Law and Education Department* (Mis), dated 30th September 1901, T.N.A.
72. *Nos. 26 & 27 Law and Education Department* (Mis), dated 23rd January, 1901, T.N.A.
73. *G.O No. 650, Law and Education Department*, 9th April 1930, T.N.A.
74. *Qaumi Report*, Vaniyambadi, Fortnightly Report, October 1926, T.N.A.
75. *Andhra Patrika*, Madras, 3rd April, 1914, T.N.A.
76. *Jaridah-i-Rozgar*, Madras, 28th April, 1914, T.N.A.
77. *G.O No. 1591, Law and Education Department*, dt. 9-9-1931, T.N.A.
78. *G.O No. 1727, Law and Education Department*, dt. 22-9-1933, T.N.A.
79. *Ibid*
80. *G.O No. 871, Law and Education Department*, dt. 27-4-1928, T.N.A.
81. *G.O No. 1414, Law and Education Department*, dt. 27-7-1928, T.N.A.
82. *G.O No. 1087, Law and Education Department*, dt. 18-9-1922, T.N.A.
83. *G.O No. 270, Education and Public Health*, dt. 5-2-1941, T.N.A.
84. *Ibid.*
85. *G.O No.115, Law and Education Department*, dt. 24-2-1911, T.N.A.

CHAPTER

Muslim Efforts and the Government Response Before and After Independence

The serious defects and the indifferent attitude of the Muslims towards Western Education received a tremendous change during the first quarter of the twentieth century. The Muslim community began to understand their flaw and moved towards Western Education. The demands of the elites of the Muslim community for more and more concessions and facilities from the Government for their people, the Muslim's demands and the Government's response towards it, their requests to give back the cancelled concessions and privileges like half fee concession and getting position in the higher classes of Government service, the submission of petitions on their grievances for redressal and the efforts to improve their educational status during the British regime and in the post independent India have been discussed in this Chapter. Though the Muslims were not fully successful in their attempts, their spirit and the positive attitude towards the English Education was an appreciable one.

At the close of the nineteenth century the British Government had cancelled some of the concessions like paying half fee by the Mohammedan children and reservation in higher class Government services to the Muslims. This news was highlighted by the newspaper 'The Mohammedan'.

Hence, the Mohammedan inhabitants of Mangalore submitted a memorandum requesting the British Government to give back the concessions cancelled by it.[1] The Muslims appealed to the Government that as a backward people in education their growing generation deserves some more concessions to encourage them in getting English Education. Their appeal was published in the Newspaper, 'The Mohammedan'. They also requested the Government to grant exemption to the Muslim students in getting positions in the higher classes of Government service and also pointed out that the concessions given already was inadequate and not equal to what Hindu brethren had been enjoying since the organization of Public service. In this regard they requested the Government to accept the recommendation made by the 'Board of Mohammedan Education.'

The above-mentioned Memorandum was submitted to the Governor of Madras to intrude upon their grievances with a hope of receiving essential help. The Muslims were expecting more concessions from the Government; in such condition taking back the half fee concession from the Mohammedan students and cancellation of reservation in getting higher class Government services gave a great disappointment to the Muslim community. The Muslim community was feeling that the concessions given were inadequate and not equal to that of the Hindus enjoying since the inception of the Public services. The Hindus paid very small amount of school fee for a very long time until they rose to high position and prosperity, while the Muslims had no such benefits left for them. It was a fact that a few Anglo-Hindustani schools for the Muslim youths were opened here and there, but no fee concession was extended to them.[2] This was made known to the Government also by the 'Board of Mohammedan Education.'

The Memorialist most earnestly prayed to the Government to provide for the education of the Muhammadans with suitable Anglo-Hindustani institutions combined with low fee structure. And they also requested that the Government should be pleased to confer on them some responsible posts such as Deputy Collector, Deputy Superintendent of Police, Tahsildar etc. giving effect to the recommendation and request of the 'Board of Muhammadan Education' at an early date, as the rising Muslim generation was sinking more and more to the depth of poverty, ignorance and distress.[3]

In reply to this Memorandum submitted by the Muslims, the Government repliẹd that, generally education among Mohammadans not received any appreciable improvement. The last report of the Director of Public Instruction showed that in some respect it went back, in spite of the very special and peculiar privileges given to this community, it was very difficult to assign reason for this but it called for the most earnest attention of the leaders of the Muslim community. Some quickest method of arousing their interest and energy would be abolishing of all special concessions and privileges![4] Generally, a favoured class is apt to become a lethargic one. The Government had already given enough concessions; no additions to them were called for. Regarding the establishment of Anglo-Hindustani institutions the Government further clarified that it had opened already many schools through out the Presidency (but they were opened to all classes). There was no necessity for establishing a special institution for Muhammadans alone. For the reservation of the higher posts which was already in the attention of the Government and the heads of the Department had been called to it on various proceedings in the bound file, so no further actions seems to be called for.[5]

The Government's reply to the Memorialists shows that the Government is disgusted with the response of the Muslims towards the efforts taken by the Government for the improvement of the education of the Muslims. The fear complex and the remarks of the Memorialists about their community seemed to be groundless. But the Government's reply to the reservation of posts in the higher classes of Government service was not acceptable and more sympathetic consideration was the need of the Muslim community. The

Government had mistaken on the economic condition of the Muslims as they were affluent community, but the fact was that they could not afford to establish Anglo-Hindustani schools of their own.

A Muslim gentleman from Valuthur of Tanjore District submitted a petition to the British Government of Madras Presidency to open an English medium school in their village for their children.[6] Another request of the same category was submitted to the Government by the Muslim Community of Kumbakonam.[7] Even though they were not successful in their attempt and request, the change of attitude took place in their minds towards English Education is perceptible here. The Memorialists and the elites of the Muslim community brought to the notice of the British Government about the condition of the rising generation which was going more and more to the depth of poverty, ignorance and distress. The above said incidents were showing the reaction and response of the community.

The All India Muslim Educational Conference was held at Madras in 1901, which tried to draw the attention of the British Government about the sad plight of the Muslim community in getting Government jobs especially of the higher posts. It also pointed out the inadequate steps to improve the condition of the Muslim community in the sphere of Education. This appeal and request had an effect because there was some response on both the sides. The Director of Public Instruction records and the Administrative Reports of the Madras Presidency bear a witness to it. After a lapse of 25 years, another All India Muslim Educational Conference proposed to be held at Madras in December 1927. The Chairman of the All India Muslim educational Conference, Madras reception Committee wrote a letter to the Secretary to Government, Law and Education Department of Madras Government to provide a review of the progress made in the education of the Muslims in the past 25 years.[8] He also requested the Government to supply the Reception Committee with G.Os on the issues such as Mappillah education in general and the appointment of a special Educational Officer for Mappillahs in particular, abolition of the half fee concession in the case of Mohammedans, grant of scholarships to Mappillas and other Musalmans and the manner of their reservation, establishment of the Mohammedan Government College at Madras on a temporary basis, special recurring grant of Rs. 30,000 made by the Government of India for Muslim education in this Presidency and the manner of its utilization from the year to year, appointment of Urdu, Persian and Arabic Munshis in Government schools and Colleges or similar aided institutions, appointment of Muslims in District Educational Councils and the recruitment of Muslims for the higher inspecting agency of the Educational Department in pursuance of the recommendations of the various educational commissions.[9]

The Chairman of the conference also requested the Government that the Director of Public Instruction through whom the Muslim officers employed in the Educational Department may be kindly instructed to offer necessary facilities in the way of the collection of the statistics required for the purposes of the conference.[10]

In response to the letter written by the Chairman of the All India Muslim Educational Conference C.Abdul Hakim Sahib, the Government supplied figures and information on the development of education of the Muslims. Instruction was given to the Director of Public Instruction to appoint Muslim officers in the Educational Department. Necessary statistics and information related to this were collected from the various quarters on Muhammadan Education.

In response to the All-India Muslim Educational Conference Chairman Abdul Hakim's request, the Government had ordered the Director of Public Instruction to furnish with the G.Os on the subjects specified and to supply the necessary statistics relating to the education of the Muhammadans to the Chairman of the All India Muslim Educational Conference.[11] The Government accordingly issued G.Os in connection with the Education of the Muslims.[12]

The G.Os issued covered more or less the subjects specified by the Chairman of the Conference. Regarding the Imperial recurring grant of Rs. 30,000 allocated for the purpose of the education of the Muslims had been discontinued after the introduction of financial reforms by the Government but all the items of expenditure which were met from the imperial grants were to be met from the Provincial funds. Regarding the appointment of Muslims in the District Educational Council, provision was already made to nominate a representative of the Muhammadan Community. About the recruitment of Muslims for the higher inspecting agency of the Educational Department, the Government was making appointments by giving due consideration to the claims of all communities and therefore there were no general orders on the subject and that the claims of Muhammadans for the appointment to the superior inspecting agency would be considered in due course.[13]

Regarding the statistics demanded by the Chairman of the conference, the Government was not clear about the request and the kind of statistics required by him. Generally, which might ordinarily be available in published reports and it was not an easy task for the departmental officials to collect fresh statistics to meet the special requirements. So, the Government replied that this was an unusual request and the statistics might have been collected from published reports and if any particular instance the figures in the reports found inadequate then the Government will clarify it.[14] The Government further said that it would be glad to consider the question of making such further statistics available as far as possible.

In regard to the recurring Imperial grant of Rs. 30,000, the Government said that the grant was originally allocated for expenditure on the following objects, Opening of two secondary schools for Mohammedans at Vellore and Trichinopoly, Opening of an Elementary Training school, Trichinopoly, Reorganization of the Mohammedans Inspecting Agency, Subsidy towards the employment of Hindustani

Munshis in certain schools, managed by the local leaders, Subsidy to the Nellore Municipal Council for raising one of its elementary schools to the Secondary Grade, Institution of special scholarship for Mohammedans, Employment of additional staff in the Madrasa-I-Azam and the Mohammedan secondary school, George Town.[15]

Soon after the reply received from the Government, C. Abdul Hakim Sahib Bahadur wrote a letter for further clarification and requested the Government once again to furnish a copy of each of the above-mentioned papers.

The Imperial grant as such had ceased after the introduction of the financial reforms and all items of expenditure, which were being met from that grant prior to the reforms, debited to provincial funds were not properly allocated and spent.

Regarding the appointment of Urdu, Persian and Arabic Munshis in Muhammadans schools and Colleges, the Chairman had invited the attention of the Government to refer the previous G.O No. 404 Educational, dated 10th May 1912. In that the Government had promised to appoint and grant subsidy to the above-mentioned posts were not given effect so far.

Regarding the request of representation of Muslims on District Educational Councils and the inspecting agency, the Government said that there were no general orders on the subjects, but it could be treated as a special case and considered soon. Like this the Chairman of the All India Muslim Educational Conference drew the attention of the Government to the various grievances related to the education of the Muslims. The Government also responded to it. Thus a mutual understanding and cordial relationship of submitting Memorandum and getting reply to the same was maintained between the Government and the Muslims. This was an appreciable change and improvement in the attitude of the Muslims when compared to the conditions prevailed in previous years.

The chief exponent of the promotion of the Education of the Muslims during the twentieth century was Justice Basheer Ahmed Sayeed Sahib. Justice Basheer was one of the great visionaries who championed the cause of the Education of the Muslims. His contribution in this regard was a significant one.

Justice Basheer Ahamed Sayeed Sahib was born at Mylapore in the city of Madras. His early education was in a village school near Siruvadi. He had his Elementary and High school education in Crane School of American Arcot Mission, Tindivanam. He graduated from Madras Christian College then situated at N.S.C. Bose Road opposite to the High Court and his special subject was Political Science.

Basheer Ahamed Sayeed got his degree in law in 1923. He joined the 'Khilafat Movement' organized by the Ali brothers (Moulana Mohammed Ali and Moulana Shoukath Ali) in 1924. Later, he joined the Congress committee under the leadership of C.R. Doss of Bengal and Srinivasa Iyenger of Madras. Till his death, he continued to be a Congressman. From 1921 to 1941 he was an active politician.[16] During this period he took active participation in the Khilafat movement and as well as in the Non Co-operation movement launched by Gandhiji.

During the year 1924 and 1926 Basheer Ahamed Sayeed was the District Congress Secretary. He was a member of All India Congress Committee until 1946. In 1926 he contested the Corporation elections and was declared elected as Councilor, Corporation of Madras against many odds. He evinced keen interest in the social, cultural, educational upgradation of the Muslim community of South India. He was for a long duration associated with the Syndicates of the Madras University, Annamalai University, Aligarh Muslim University and other social organizations in the South. He was keen on establishing a College for Muslim boys as early as 1946. As Secretary of the Muslim Educational Association of Southern India, he was instrumental in purchasing 31 acres land in Peter's Road, Royapettah in Madras with great difficulty. As the Muslim Educational Association of South India did not have sufficient funds for this purpose, he negotiated a loan and finally he purchased the land. Immediately, he sought affiliation for a College to be managed by the M.E.A.S.I in Madras University. In this connection, Dr. A.L. Mudaliar, the then Vice-Chancellor of Madras University was of great assistance to him in the matter of getting affiliation. Finally, the College, which he himself named as the 'New College', came into existence in 1951 and was inaugurated by the then Governor-General of India late C. Rajagopalachari. Mean while Justice Basheer Ahamed Sayeed was elevated to the Bench of the Madras High Court in July 1949.

Basheer Ahamed Sayeed Sahibs' talented and dedicated wife, who was very much interested to uplift of the Muslim women, constantly reminded him that he should start a College for Muslim women. The immediate reason for her suggestion was the closure of the Government Muslim Women's College in Madras City. This was a great shock to the Muslim Community and the time had come to fulfill their dream of starting a College for Women in general and for Muslim Women in particular. A society under the title of 'The Southern India Educational Trust' was registered on 23rd October 1951 under the Societies Registration Act XXI of 1860. Moulana Abdul Haq and Dr. A.L. Mudaliar and other friends of his in the educational field encouraged him and gave him the moral support. The institution viz., 'S.I.E.T Women's College' came into being on seventh july1955. It was a red lettered day in the History of Madras City when Pandit Jawaharlal Nehru, the then Prime Minister of India, laid the foundation for the College and Moulana Abdul Kalam Azad laid the foundation for the First Hall of Residence, which was named after him. The strength of the College that day was 106 students with 21 members of staff.[17]

It was not an easy task to found a College from scratch, but he was a highly resourceful and talented person who had dedicated himself to the cause of education and he left no stone unturned in order to improve the financial status of this infant institution. For this purpose, he visited various places of South East Asia and East Africa with a view to collect funds. His contact with the Ministry of Education, Government of India, and U.G.C had helped him get affiliation for various subjects. During a short span of time, the College developed into a Post Graduate Institution and later a Research Centre.

The Southern India Education Trust (during his life time) was the hub of immense cultural activity in the City of Madras. One dignitary after another, both National and International visited this institution due to the efforts and perseverance of this man of vision and action. Some of the dignitaries who have graced this institution with their august presence were his Imperial Majesty of Iran, King Hussain of Jordon and Abdul Kamal Nasser the President of Egypt. Ambassadors of various nations including China have visited this institution.[18] Slowly and gradually he was preparing the ground for elevating this institution into a university. Had he lived, this dream of his would have been fulfilled. He passed away on the 7th February 1984.

The name of S.I.E.T. College has been changed to Justice Basheer Ahamed Sayeed Women's College from April 1984 to perpetuate the memory of its founder Justice Basheer Ahamed Sayeed. In the year 1984 in his memory, the Justice Basheer Ahamed Sayeed Memorial Matriculation Higher Secondary Boys School was started by the members of the Executive Council of the S.I.E.T.[19]

Basheer Ahmed Sayeed's services to the cause of Education to the Muslims started from the British period. In the year 1928, he wrote a petition to the Government of Madras Presidency, Law and Education Department and drew the attention of the Government to the Educational development of the Muslim community. In his petition he pointed out the inadequacy of the number of scholarships to Muslim students in the Collegiate and secondary Education. He questioned the reducing of the allotment of Rs. 2,27,600 for scholarships (in general) and drew the attention of the Government to discuss the inadequacy of the number of scholarships to Muslim students in the Collegiate and the Secondary Education and urged the Government to increase the same.[20]

To Sayeed's letter, the Government replied in an elaborate manner, that the Government was giving special scholarships to the Pupils of the Muhammadan community studying in Colleges and schools. To the Boys studying in Secondary level, there were 25 scholarships commencing from the last form and continuing throughout the whole of the secondary course. The value of these scholarships was Rs. 3 a month in each forms I to III and Rs.6 a month in each of forms IV to VI. They were tenable by certain special classes of Mohammedans. 83 additional scholarships awardable to poor Mohammedan pupils on marked ability. 55 of these were of the value of Rs.3 each and tenable in forms I to III. The remaining 28 were of the value of Rs. 6 each and tenable in forms IV to VI. 4 collegiate scholarships of the value of Rs. 9 each in the intermediate classes and Rs. 14 in the B.A classes. In addition to this one scholarship of Rs.1 a month was also available for the final B.A., Honours class. For Girls, in secondary level– 63 scholarships and 30 guardian allowances for Hindu and Muhammadan widows were awarded. Four scholarships of the value of Rs. 3 each in form I to III and of Rs. 6 in forms IV to VI were given in the Hobart training school, Royapettah.[21]

In addition to the above, Mohammedan pupils were given preferences in the award of the general scholarships available to all classes. It should also be noted that under rule 92 of the Madras Educational Rules, poor Mohammedan pupils need to pay only half the rate of the fees in secondary schools and Colleges. In order to that the Managers of the private institutions were readily extending this concession, the Grant in Aid code provided that the Government should make good to Managers the loss in the income occurred by the grant of the half fee concession.[22]

The Government said that from the above-mentioned factors, it could not be seriously contended that the benefits, which the Muhammadans were receiving in the way of scholarships, were not adequate.

To achieve this objects an Imperial grant of Rs. 30,000 was allocated to the Director of Public Instruction (Reference G.O 332 Education). But this measure was not given effect, because education was made as a State subject as per the request of newly formed Justice Party Government and the introduction of educational reforms there by. The Imperial grant was discontinued but all that items of expenditure which were to be met from the Imperial grants were met from provincial funds.[23]

When the 15th session of the Muslim Educational Conference was held in Madras, a new Organisation, especially meant for the South Indian Muslims was formed which was called as 'The Muslim Educational Association of South India.'[24] Its aim was to give educational opportunity to the Muslims of South. It is abbreviated as MEASI. MEASI has been playing a vital role in the promotion of the education of the Muslims for the past hundred years. It is still performing its service in shaping the Muslim students in the field of education.

During 1940s, Malang Ahamed Batcha was the President and Justice Basheer Ahamed Sayeed was the Secretary of MEASI. As the Secretary of MEASI Justice Basheer Ahamed Sayeed wrote a letter to Sir Thomas Austin, Adviser to the Governor of Madras representing certain matter such as, the early establishment of a separate College for Muslim women in the city of Madras and the construction of a hostel attached to the said College, the institution of B.Sc pass and Hon's courses in the Mohammedan College, the appointment of a Muslim Deputy Director as and when Khan Bahadur Moulvi Mohamed Sahib retires, the raising of the scale of salary for the post of the Principal of the Government Mohammedan College, the admission of Muslim students in Government Colleges, the establishment of a high school in Perambur area in Madras, the revision of the scales of salary for the Primary, Secondary and L.T or B.T grade teachers and the early construction of quarters for Muslim women teachers posted to high schools in the Mofussil.[25]

Basheer Ahmed Sayeed also requested the Adviser to Governor Sir Thomas Austin to give an appointment to discuss the above mentioned matters. The representation made by Mr. Basheer Ahmed Sayeed was given due importance, consultation were done on the points raised with the department concerned and the following reply was sent to him.

In reply to a similar representation from the Mohammedan Educational Association of South India, the Government requested the Director Public Instruction to consult the Madras university in the first instance and if the opening of College classes was justified, to examine the practicability of providing the necessary accommodation in the premises of the Hobart secondary and Training school for Mohammedan women, Royapettah.[26] Basheer Ahmed Sayeed who was the Honorary Secretary of the Mohammedan Educational Association of South India had received this reply.

In reply to a similar representation, the Mohammedan Educational Association of South India was informed that this item had been put down in the five year post-war plan which the Government proposed to implement as early as possible.

The admission of Muslim students had been made available in all Government Colleges. The revision and raising pay scales for the teachers, in general accepted, as principle and a Committee would be formed. All other matters found in the representation would be considered in consultation with department concerned.[27]

Justice Basheer Ahmed Sayeed wrote another letter to Honourable T.S. Avinasilingam Chettiar, the Minister of Education, Madras Presidency, in which he clarified his statement made by him at the public meeting of the Muslims held at the Lawley Hall, Mount Road, Madras on the 11th January 1947, under the auspices of Muslim Educational Association of South India, Madras. The statement was not fully reported in the press. He had taken this step to keep the minister acquainted with the full facts. He looked forward to hearing from the Minister, and the steps he propose to take to allay the feelings of the Muslim community in the matter of so vitally a problem as Muslim education.[28]

This public meeting of the Muslim citizens of Madras was convened under the auspices of the Muslim Educational Association of Southern India. It was well known to the people of this province that the Muslim Educational Association of Southern India was the premier association, which had been working for the social and educational advancement of the Muslim community of this province for more than a century. This association could claim without the least fear of any contradiction that but for the incessant activities of this association in many directions, the progress of the Muslim Community would have been different.

Besides its other activities, this Association was awarding every year, about 300 scholarships to poor and deserving Muslim students, thanks to the munificence of the members of the community. Justice Basheer Ahmed Sayeed proudly said that this number was greater than what was the Government awarding every year to the Muslims in this province. Nevertheless, it remained an undeniable fact that the Muslim community in this prφvince has still to make much way, if it has to take its rightful place in the social, economic and political life of this country in future.

The object of this meeting was therefore to consider the "Educational future of the Muslims of this Province" in all its aspects and to bring home to the members of the Muslim community and the Government of that day, the urgent and essential needs of the community in the sphere of education. Even though it was too late to improve upon the community and the Government, a sound education was the sure foundation for all the future development of any community in any country. The Government and the community must know that no planning for the future development of the country in any sphere would be sufficient unless and until the education of the youth of the community has been well planned and the plan had to be worked out on sound and proper lines.

It had all been the endeavour of the Muslim Educational Association of Southern India to point out to the Government on behalf of the Muslim community what could be the scheme of education that would be most healthy and conducive to the rapid progress of the community. The then Ministry was most ignorant of the real needs of the Muslim Community. The Association considered that it would be the duty of this association to represent the entire Muslim community of this province to educate the Honourable Minister of Education and his colleagues about the requirements of the community for its full growth and development.[29]

Justice Basheer Ahmed Sayeed further wrote in his letter, "Therefore in the fitness of things that through this public meeting and in unerring terms, it should be brought home to the Government, in the first place, that the education of the Muslims, who are in a minority and who are economically poor and educationally backward in this province, is and should be the special responsibility and the foremost may be welcome in this direction, the community cannot depend upon private effort for its educational progress, and that the Government should always bear the entire cost of educating both the sexes of the community in all grades and types of education."[30]

In the next place, it was necessary that the Government should be warned once and for all that no scheme of education, however well planned and well conceived it might be, would neither be acceptable to the Muslims of that province nor would not and could not have accepted any position to reconcile themselves to any situation, wherein, their historic and cultural importance is not recognized and their right to an adequate share in this services and to effective and adequate representation on the various bodies and organizations that have been and are being set up, has not been conceded."

Basheer Ahmed Sayeed had expressed, it was most unfortunate that, by reason of the many ill-conceived declarations of the policy and the several acts of commission and omission on the part of the Congress Ministry in power during 1947, especially in the sphere of education, and in regard to educational institutions, the confidence of the Muslims of this province had been rudely shaken and their suspicions had been roused as to whether the then Ministry means and intends well by the minority community, at all.

Quoting only a few instances about the attitude of the Ministry, he remarked that the Government was refusing to recognize Urdu as the national and cultural language of the Muslims. The Government was declining to make or secure adequate provision for the teaching of Persian and Urdu in institutions to which Muslims were forced to resort to and a large section of the Muslims on seeking to compel to learn through a language, which was not their mother tongue. Basheer Ahmed Sayeed had also pointed out that the Government was declining to constitute a separate advisory board and a separate Directorate for Muslim education. The Government had failed to recognize the need for separate institutions for the men and women of the Muslim community. It rejected unceremoniously all suggestions and requests of the Association (MEASI) for the opening of more Schools and Colleges for Muslim men and women.

Basheer Ahamed Sayeed further pointed out that the Government had dismissed Urdu Munshis from schools even in the middle of the term, on the ground that Urdu is not the regional language of the area concerned, while retaining other non-regional languages in the same school, such as Sanskrit, Hindi and Telugu, not withstanding the protests of the Association. The Government had failed to give adequate representations to the Muslim community on the reconstituted S.S.L.C. Board. There were only two Muslims out of the total strength of 25 on the Board in spite of remonstrance from this Association. When the Provincial Advisory Board of Education was constituted the Government had failed to appoint an adequate number of Muslims on the board. There were only 2 Muslims on this Board out of a total strength of 29 in spite of representations made by this Association. The Government had refused to appoint a fact finding commission to enquire into and settle the controversial points between the Government and the representatives of the community on the question of recognizing Urdu as a regional language, to acquire suitable sites for the location of schools and hostels intended for Muslims and refusing to assign Government wasteland in the Government house compound for the construction of a hostel for Muslim men and women in the city of Madras, refusing to concede the principle accepted by the former Government (Congress Ministry formed before independence) that religious instruction should form an integral part of the school curriculum for the education of Muslim boys and girls and refusing to recognize the dire need for a greater number of scholarships to encourage higher education among Muslim women and men.

On the failure to afford sufficient inducements and adequate facilities to attract a larger number of Muslims to the teaching profession to make up for the dearth of Muslim men and women teachers and above all, the Government had declined to frame a scheme of expansion of education among the Muslims, after an investigation into the causes of stagnation and the actual needs of the community by a commission of experts on Muslim education appointed for the purpose.[31]

The above factors simply confirm the grave misgivings of the Muslim community about the good intention of the Ministry and its sincerity of purpose towards the educational future of the Muslim community. To add fuel to fire the Government issued a questionnaire on the Reorganization of Education in the Province, which had simply aggravated the situation. The questionnaire did not deal with any respect of

Muslim education as such; nevertheless, the association had furnished its answers to the questions, of course reserving and its right to frame and submit a comprehensive scheme for the expansion of Muslim Education in due course. The Honourable Minister had kindly acknowledged the receipt of the answers but had observed that the same was received too late, meaning thereby that he did not propose to consider the same as serving any purpose.

Being an Urdu speaking Muslim Justice Basheer Ahmed Sayeed gave much stress and importance to the Urdu language and problem of the Urdu speaking Muslims. He had failed to deal the subject i.e. education of the Muslims in general. He had simply forgotten that among the Muslim population of Madras Presidency two-third of the people have Tamil as their mother tongue. Anyhow, his remarks on the Government policies and attitude were meaningful. As the pioneer of the cause of the education of the Muslims, his spirit and interest shown were highly appreciable. The attitude of the then Ministry towards Muslim education was a vital problem of the community which was acknowledged on all hands to be a 'Special Interest' of the Muslims, requiring statutory safeguards and protection.

For the statement made by the Honorary Secretary of the Muslim Educational Association of Southern India, Madras, dated 14th January 1947, the Governor's Secretary replied that with regard to Educational needs of the Muslims he liked to refer to the D.O from the P.S.G note of 5th February 1947. Allegations had been made against the good intentions of the Ministry and its sincerity of purpose towards the Educational future of the Muslim Community. The previous Congress Ministry of 1938 recognised Urdu as national cultural language of the Muslims. The Government had permitted the use of the mother tongue as the medium of instruction in secondary school level. Even though there was no appreciable progress made in this direction and Urdu could not be considered as a regional language in this Province, because of the representation made by the Urdu speaking people, the

Government had allowed the medium of instruction in the schools in areas where the mother tongue of the Muslim pupils was Urdu and also to introduce Urdu and Arabic as second languages in schools in those areas. Under the S.S.L.C scheme, Urdu and Arabic were permitted as second languages as group 'A' and also as optional subjects under group 'C'. The Governor's Secretary had pointed out many of the concessions and privileges given to them by the Government and rejected the request of appointing a separate commission to settle the question of recognizing Urdu as the regional language.[32]

Regarding the Muslim members on the Provincial Advisory Board of Education, there were two Muslim members on the Provincial Advisory Board of education, Justice Yahya Ali and Mr. Basheer Ahmed. The representation made by the association for increasing the number of Muslim members on the Board had already been considered, so it was not necessary to change the constitution of the Board. He said that as the number of schools specially intended for Muslims was small, there would seem to be hardly any justification for the immediate increase of members or constitution of a separate Advisory Board or a separate Directorate for Muslim education.[33]

The Governor's secretary also added that the suggestion to set up parallel and separate system of education for Muslims which was likely to retard rather than help the progress of Muslims and that the proposal was also impracticable on financial grounds. The suggestion was not accepted. They considered that in places where there were no separate schools, it would be sufficient if facilities were given for the education of the Muslims in non-Muslim schools. The policy was maintained. It was not proposed to open any new schools in 1947-48. The proposal was deferred on financial grounds and the same reason was also applicable to the opening of new colleges in general and for Muslims in particular. As regard to the opening of a college for Muslim women, in Madras, the Government had already agreed as a post war plan (Second World War) with effect from 1946-47.

Accordingly, the college was opened in the buildings of Government Hobart Secondary Training School, Royapettah and the same would be shifted after constructing permanent buildings for the college.[34]

For all other representations made by the Association, the Government had given a satisfactory reply and expressed the difficulties before it in immediate implementation of the certain requests of the Muslims. Regarding the increase of scholarships for the higher education of the Muslim men and women, the Government said that it had already provided a sufficient number of residential scholarships for men and women, but as no Muslim Mappilla girls were studying in the Government College of Madras, it was not sanctioned. With regard to the appointment of a Committee of Experts on Muslim education, the Government deemed it to be not necessary. The Government was always ready to hear the Muslim members' demands and proposals for the advancement of their education.

The efforts of Muslim on the development of the education of their community were far advanced when compared to the state of condition in the beginning of the twentieth Century. To those representations and demands made by the Muslims, the British Government and the Congress Ministry formed before Independence gave due regard and considered positively as far as possible. But after Independence, the Government records have no mention of the education of the Muslims. It seems that the education of the Muslims was not dealt under a separate topic.

Since the modern education was introduced in India to meet the needs of the British Raj, its progress had been restricted and its character from the standpoint of the progress of Indian people was unsatisfactory. Since the main purpose of the inauguration of modern education was to supply the English knowing personnel to the British apparatus, mass education of the Indians was not seriously viewed. After a century of British rule, 94 per cent of the Indian population remained illiterate in 1911 and 92 per cent in 1931. The number of students receiving education in the primary and secondary schools amounted 33.5 million i.e. only 4.9 per cent of the entire population in 1935. It increased 0.5 per cent in 1941-42. The number of students in higher educational institution was 1,59,254 in1942. It was the general condition of the education of the Indians.[35] In the case of Muslims the degree of illiteracy was more than their counterparts. The illiteracy resulted in ignorance among the Muslims, which inevitably obstructed social, political and economic progress.

The Indian Nationalist Muslims criticized the Government for insufficient expenditure on the education of the Muslims. This condition was further worsened after Independence. The newly formed independent Indian Government was very busy with internal calamites. It gave utmost priority to the unification of scattered Princely States under one Union Government. The Nationalist Muslim leaders and the educated Muslims concentrated on the Independence movement. After Independence they could not put forward the same demands and trials to get more concessions and facilities from the Indian Union Government because of the change of policy of the Government. The indigenous Indian Government adopted a secular policy and stopped measures as was taken by the British Government on religious ground. Instead it implemented welfare measures like promotion of education on caste basis. The scheduled class and the scheduled tribes, who were suppressed for centuries together, were given priority as a social justice. Likewise, other backward classes were also given concessions and facilities. Muslims were considered as one of the forward communities of India. However, another category of division was introduced by the Indian Government on religious ground. Muslims and Christians are brought under religious minority community. On this basis, some concessions and rights have been granted to the Muslims. But in due course, this system received several changes in the various States of India according to the will and pleasure of the State Government.

Muslim Educational Association of Southern India

The Fifteenth annual Session of the All Indian Mohammedan Education Conference was held in Madras in 1901 when it was proposed to establish this Association. The Association was incorporated, as No.18 of 1905-06 under the societies Act XXI of 1860 and the Founder President was Lord Boddam.

Till late 1940s the Association was mainly awarding educational Scholarship and hostel accommodation to Muslim Students. The early stalwarts behind this Association were Hameed Sait Sahib, B.A., Lt., (Alig), Nawab Syed Mohamed Sahib (Grandson of Tippu Sultan), Justice Sir Abdul Rahim Sahib, Sir Mohamed Habibullah Sahib, Sir Mohamed Usman Sahib, Hajee Jamal Mohamed Sahib, Janab Malang Ahamed Batcha Sahib and Quaid-e-Milath M. Mohamed Ismail Sahib.[36]

In 1947, Janab Moulvi Nazeer Hussain Sahib became the president and his foresight and acumen ushered a new era to this Association and he along with Justice Basheer Ahamed Sayeed Sahib, Janab A. Haji Mohamed Ubaidullah Sahib and other took a bold decision to establish 'THE NEW COLLEGE.'[37] Thus, this Muslim Minority College came into existence in 1951, at the present campus.

The institution grew bigger day by day and was led by community heads like M.S.A. Majid Sahib, A.K.A. Abdus Samad Sahib, A.A.Rasheed Sahib, T. Abdul Wahid Sahib and M. Mohamed Hashim Sahib, who were ably assisted by A.J. Abdul Razak Sahib and K.V.M.Abdul Kareem Sahib. Presidents of India Dr. Rajendra Prasad, Dr. Zakir Huissain and Dr. Mr. Fakruddin Ali Ahamed and Prime Ministers Shrimathi Indira Gandhi and Shri Rajiv Gandhi had visited the Institution.[38]

Today, this is the foremost Muslim Minority Institution in Tamil Nadu catering to the needs of the community imparting education to over 6000 students. The following institutions cropped up due to the efforts of this Association, the New College (1951), MEASI Matriculation Higher (1985), New College Institute of Management (1987), MEASI

Charitable Trust (1992), MEASI Computer Academy (1992), Institute of Research in soil Biology and Biotechnology (1995), MEASI Academy of Architecture (1997), MEASI Urdu Academy (1998), MEASI Institute of Technology (2002).The philanthropic attitude of the Muslim Community towards its welfare and upgradation maintained this Association in good stead.

The All-India Muslim Educational Conference session was held at Cathedral Garden, Teynampet in Mount road from December 27 to 31, 1901. It was presided over by Mr. Justice Hungerford Tudor Boddam. In accordance a resolution passed at this All India Mohammedan educational conference on 28th December, 1901, the "Mohammedan Educational Association of South India" was established in January, 1902. The name was later changed as the "Muslim Educational Association of South India" in 1946.[39]

Justice Boddam was the Founder and the President of the Association. He infused courage, confidence and spirit of self-reliance in the Community. From the beginning the MEASI continued to award scholarships to Muslim students.

The construction work of the Boddam Hostel in George Town was started in August 1915. It was functioning in 1981 with the grant received from the Government and with the funds of the Association. The Hostel was useful to the Muslim students coming from various parts of Presidency and studying in various Colleges in the city. The hostel celebrated its Silver Jubilee on 6th and 7th of May 1935.

In 1948, the Association purchased 12 acres of land with a two storeyed building, then originally, knows as 'Tawkar's Garden' and later as 'Limbidi Garden' at 49, Peters Road, Royapettah for a sum of Rs. 4,36,000 in the name of MEASI and the office of the Association was shifted from Boddam Hostel building, Singara Naick St, George town to Association Garden, Royapettah on 11th August, 1949.[40]

After the Independence the Government changed the Policy with regard to the admission in the Government Muslim

College. Under the new policy, the proportion of Muslims in the matter of admission, which was hither to 75 per cent, was reduced to just 7 per cent. The strength of the Muslim staff of the College was also reduced and the Government Muslim College was renamed as Government Arts College. Consequently, in this Government Arts College the Muslims were not given preference. In these circumstances the Muslims rose to the occasion and established their own Colleges in the various districts of Tamil Nadu. The undermentioned colleges with a view to impart higher education for Muslims were started after the independence, mostly between 1950 and 1970 by the philanthropic munificence of the generous hearted people of the Muslim community.

The New College

The idea of starting a College under the Association, which was abandoned in 1916, was revived in 1948. In October 1948, the first application of the New College was made to the University of Madras. A second application was submitted to the University in October 1950. Dr. A. Lakshmanaswamy Mudaliyar, the then vice Chancellor of Madras University and Several eminent educationists inspected the buildings and the playground in the Association garden and granted recognition to the New College.

The College was named by Justice Basheer Ahamed Sayeed as the 'New College' after the model of the New College in Oxford. The New College was inaugurated by Sir Rajagopalachari, the then Home Minister of the Government of India on 2nd July, 1951. The College was started with only intermediate classes with 200 students in Humanities.

In 1952-53, Quaid-e-Millath Alhaj M. Mohamed Ismail Sahib, M.P., the President of the Indian Union Muslim League led a delegation consisting of Janab Jamal Mohamed Sahib, Secretary, Jamal Mohamed College, Trichy and Janab M.S.A.Majid Sahib, Honorary Secretary the New College, Madras to the far Eastern Countries to raise funds for the infant institutions. With the fund raised in the far Eastern

Countries, the Science Block was constructed at a cost of Rs. 1, 08,000. It was named as 'Burma-Malaya Block'. The New block was declared open by Honorable Sri K. Kamaraj Nadar, the chief Minister of the Government of Madras on 18th July 1954. Pre-University classes were started in 1956 and in 1957, the three year degree courses came into being B.A. History, Economic, B.Sc. Zoology, Mathematics and Chemistry Courses were started in 1957 with the starting of Degree courses The New College became a first grade institution. B.Sc. Physics was started in 1960. New courses in Under Graduates and Post Graduates were started in due course. Many M.Phil, and Ph.D., research courses were also introduced in the college.

The Constitution of India has guaranteed Fundamental Rights under Articles 26 to 30 to establish educational institutions, trusts and associations to the religious minorities of India. In exercising these Fundamental Rights, the State Governments granted permission to the Muslims all over India to establish their own trusts and educational institutions wherever necessary. As a result of this good measure the Muslims started various educational societies, trusts and associations for the promotion of Higher education in Tamil Nadu. A number of schools and colleges were started in the places where the Muslim community living in a large number.

Islamiah College, Vaniyambadi

The Muslims in North Arcot district established a society called 'Vaniyambadi Muslim Educational Society' in 1903. It was started with the intention of translating Sir Syed Ahamed Khan's message in to action. i.e. the spreading of Modern education among the Muslim masses.

The Vaniyambadi Muslim Educational Society was registered in 1905 and soon under its auspices the Islamiah Elementary School was started. The phenomenal growth of the School was due to the dedicated service and leadership of Janab T. Hajee Baduruddin Sahib, Janab Malang Hayath Batcha Sahib, Janab T.Ameenudin Sahib and Janab Malang

Ahamed Batcha Sahib. The full-fledged Islamiah High Schools came into being in 1912.

The Vaniyambadi Muslim Educational Society decided to establish Islamiah College and the foundation stone of the College was laid by his Excellency Lord Pentland, the then Governor of Madras Province, in 1916. The College was started in 1919 with the help of Muslim Philanthropists. Nawab C. Abdul Hakeem Sahib was one of the Philanthropists, who gave a munificent donation of Rs. 50,000 to the Society.

Jamal Mohammed College, Trichy

Jamal Mohamed was a great educationist. He served for the development of education among the Muslims of Tamil Nadu. He was not only a great educationalist but also a great freedom fighter. He took part in the freedom movement of our country and he was a close associate of the father of our nation, Mahatma Gandhi.

With the tireless efforts of Janab N.M. Kaja Mian Rowther and Janab Hajee M. Jamal Mohamed Sahib and other member of the Majlis-ul-Ulema (assembly of the learned), Tiruchirapalli and the Jamal Mohammed College was founded in 1951.

Khadir Mohideen College, Adirampattinam

The Khadir Mohideen College was founded by the trust Known as M.K.N. Matharasa of Adirampattinam. The trust was created by the great philanthropist Janab Late Haji Khadir Mohideen and his munificent brothers. The Late Haji S.M.S. Shaik Jalaludeen founded the Khadir Mohideen College in 1955.

Justice Basheer Ahamed Sayeed Women's College, Madras

The Southern India Education Trust was founded in 1951 by Justice Basheer Ahamed Sayeed. The Southern India Education Trust Started the Justice Basheer Ahamed Sayeed College in 1955.

Hajee Karutha Rowther Howdia College, Uthamapalayam

S. Mohamed Meeran, popularly known as Hajee Karutha Rowther was the founder of Hajee Karutha Rowther Howdia College. Hajee Karutha Rowther was a freedom fighter. As a part of Khilafat Movement he organised a Conference at Uthamapalayam on 11th September 1922. In July 1956, the College was formally inaugurated by Sri. K.Kamaraj, the then Chief Minister of Madras State.

C. Abdul Hakeem College, Melvisharam

The Melvisharam Muslim Educational Society was founded in 1919 by C. Abdul Hakeem Sahib. Abdul Hakeem Sahib's dream of establishing a College at Melvisharam came true on 8th July 1965, when C. Abdul Hakeem College was established.

Muqyyath Sha Sirguru Wakf Board College, Madurai

Janab M. Heera Sahib and Janab M. Abdul Khader, Social workers of Madurai mooted the idea of starting a College and spearheaded it to a Success. Janab H.K. Ghazi, I.A.S, the then Special officer for Wakfs and Janab S.J. Sadiq Basha, the then Minister for Wakfs extended their official patronage. The role of the Wakf Board in the establishment of the College is inestimable.

Mazharul Uloom College, Ambur

Mazharul Uloom College was founded at Ambur, North Arcot Ambedkar District in the year 1969 by the Ambur Muslim Educational Society.

Dr. Zakhir Hussain College, Ilayangudi

The public of Ilayangudi and its Surrounding areas, with an intention of running a College at Ilayangudi, founded a Society by a name, the Ilayangudi College Society. The Society, with the help of public and philanthropists started the College on 1970.

Sadakathullah Appa College, Tirunelveli

The task of removing ignorance and illiteracy among the Muslim of Tirunelveli District was begun by the Muslim Orphanage Committee, Palayamkottai. The torch-bearers of Muslim Community and Muslim Philanthropists contributed a lot towards the establishment of College. The Sadakathullah Appa College was started on 1st July 1971.

The Quaid-e-Milleth College, Madras

The Quaid-e-Milleth Educational and Social Trust was established on 29th January 1974. The trust established the Quaid-e-Milleth College on 24-07-1975 at Medavakkam, Madras.

Muslim Arts College, Thiruvithancode

In 1981, the cause of the education for Muslims was taken by the Muslim Educational Society. The society started the Muslim Arts College in 1982.

The Thassim Beevi Abdul Kader College for Women, Kilakarai, Ramanathapuram District

Thassim Beevi Abdul Kader College for Women was sponsored by the Seethakathi Trust. It was established in the year 1988. There are 52 members of staff with 7 undergraduate courses and 4PG courses; there are about 650 students on the roll.

Mohamed Sathak College for Arts and Science, Sholinganallur, Madras

Mohamed Sathak College of Arts and Science was started by 'The Mohamed Sathak Trust.' It is a public, charitable and educational body, established in 1973, by the philanthropic Mohamed Sathak family of Kilakarai. The College was started on 1991.Besides these Arts and science Colleges many number of Muslim institutions like Engineering and Technical institutions are functioning.

Apart from the above-mentioned higher educational institutions, a number of self financed Arts and Science colleges, Polytechnics and Engineering colleges were also established by the Muslims. Because of the latest policy of Privatisation of the educational institutions of the Tamil Nadu Government, mushrooms like self-financed institutions have been founded by the people of different communities. While making Privatisation of education, the quality of the education and the standard of the students need to be taken into consideration by which we could maintain a healthy atmosphere in the sphere of education.

REFERENCES

1. *The Muhammadan (Newspaper)* dated 11th and 14th March, 1901.
2. *Memorandum of the Muslims of Mangalore submitted to the Governor*, dated 27th August, 1901, Tamil Nadu Archives (T.N.A).
3. *Ibid.*
4. *C. No 1211, Reply of the Government*, dated 24th September, 1901, T.N.A.
5. *Ibid.*
6. *No.115, Law and Education Department (Mis),* dated 24th February, 1911, T.N.A.
7. *No.198, Law Department and Education (Press),* dated 4th May, 1911.
8. *The All India Muslim Educational Conference,* Madras Reception Committee, letter dated 29th August, 1927.
9. *Ibid.*
10. *Ibid.*
11. *C No. 4271, Law and Education Department*, dated 28th September, 1927.
12. *G.O No. 376 Education*, dated 9th March, 1923, *G.O No. 759 Education*, dated 1st July, 1920, Copies of scholarship notifications, *G.O No. 820 Education*, dated 24th June, 1918, *G.O No. 1053 Education*, dated 10th September, 1914, T.N.A.
13. *C No. 4271, Law and Education Department*, dated 28th September, 1927, T.N.A.

14. *Ibid.*
15. *Letter No.1882, Law and Education Department*, dated 30th September, 1927, T.N.A.
16. Justice Basheer Ahmed Sayeed College for Women, *Diary, 2003-04.*
17. *Ibid.*
18. *Ibid.*
19. *Ibid.*
20. *Letter No. 1185, Law and Education Department*, dated 6th March, 1928, T.N.A.
21. *G.O. No. 755, Law and Education Department*, dated 6th March, 1928, T.N.A.
22. *G.O. No. 919, Law and Education Department*, dated 30th April, 1928, T.N.A.
23. *Ibid.*
24. *MEASI Souvenir*, 101st Annual Report, dated 31st March, 2003.
25. *Letter No. G. 180/45, MEASI* dated 25th August, 1945.
26. *G.O. No 1480, Law and Education Department*, dated 19th September, 1945, T.N.A.
27. *G.O No. 1652, Law and Education Department*, dated 18th October, 1945, T.N.A.
28. *Letter No. 9/47-19, MEASI* dated 14th January, 1947.
29. *S. No. 4238 B1/47, Education and Public Health Department*, dated 21st January, 1947. (Statement of Justice Basheer Ahmed Sayeed, Lawley Hall, Madras dated 11th January, 1947), T.N.A.
30. *Ibid.*
31. *Ibid.*
32. *D.O. No. 179-C/47-2, Education and Public health department*, dated 20th January, 1947, T.N.A.
33. *Ibid.*
34. *Ibid.*
35. Desai, A.R., *Social Background of Indian Nationalism*, Bombay, 1948, p.153, T.N.A.
36. *MEASI Souvenir*, 101st Annual Report, dated 31st March, 2003.
37. *The New College Golden Jubilee Celebrations Souvenir*, 2001-02.
38. *Ibid.*
39. *MEASI Souvenir*, 101st Annual Report, dated 31st March, 2003.
40. *Ibid.*

CHAPTER

Muslim Philanthropic Efforts and Education in Tiruchirappalli and Thanjavur Districts

After the independence of India, the Union Government and the Government of the States began to follow the policy of 'Secularism'. They shaped their policy towards the promotion of education to the people of India on that basis. However the Government of India extended minority rights to the minority religious groups of India to establish and govern their own educational institutions. The percentage of admission hitherto given to the Muslim students in the Government colleges was reduced considerably. The Government Muslim College at Madras was renamed as Government Arts College. Under these circumstances the Muslim Community awakened and began to establish educational institutions for the benefit of their society.

In 1950, absolutely there were no higher educational institutions in the coastal region of Thanjavur district and as far as Tiruchirappalli district is concerned, there were only a few Christian institutions and no Muslim institution was there. There were thousands of aspirants for higher education belonging to the backward, socially oppressed poor class both in Muslim and Hindu communities. It was impossible to get admission into the then existing institutions, which were far, and a few. It was also very hard to get admission in the desired branches of study. The need for more educational institutions and the sad plight of students who aspired in vain for higher education had been agitating the minds of the philanthropists and educationists of the Muslim community. The then prevalent social and educational conditions of the vast minority of the people of the state including Muslims were highly deplorable. Under these circumstances the Muslim philanthropic efforts in Tiruchirappalli and Thanjavur districts were destined to rescue the thousands of poor students.

In the coastal region of Thanjavur district the literacy rate was very low especially of the Muslim community. To eradicate mass illiteracy prevailing in this remote area, Haji S.M.S. Shaik Jalaludeen, who was an orthodox Muslim in costume, but a cosmopolitan to the core in his outlook, with farsightedness diverted the wealth of the M.K.N. (Mohammed Salih, Khadir Mohideen and Naina Mohammed) Madrasa Trust to the modern education also. He understood the sad plight of the poor students of this region for education and took the responsibility of educating them. He started educational institutions especially the Khadir Mohideen College to serve the utmost need of the people of this coastal region. In Tiruchirappalli district, the cause of the education was served by the late Hazrat Syed Murthuza, late Haji N.M. Khajamian Rawther and late Haji M. Jamal Mohammed Sahib who determined to meet the challenges in establishing Muslim educational institutions and got great success in their attempts. Even though there were rich people in other communities in these areas only the Muslim minority philanthropists came forward to shoulder the social responsibility of educating the poor and downtrodden of their areas is a fact accompli. Next to Vaniyambadi Muslims of the North Arcot district the Tiruchirappalli district Muslims had played a predominant role in the promotion of the education of the Muslims of Tamil Nadu. This Chapter mainly focuses on the above aspect of the study.

The State's attempt to encourage education began only after the first half of the nineteenth century. The position of education in the Tiruchirappalli district during the close of the first quarter of the nineteenth century was indeed much disheartening. Public Instruction was not considered then, the duty of the state even though the local Chieftains sometimes took pains to patronize it.[1] Sir Thomas Munroe, the Governor of Madras Presidency, conducted an enquiry throughout the Presidency to assess the condition of the education in 1822, which revealed the existence of several Schools and institutions in the district. These Schools were Pyall Schools to teach the young to write, read and recite while the Colleges were mostly Veda Patasalas, attended generally by Brahmin boys, who were taught the sciences of grammar, logic and literature. However, the peculiar nature of the instruction imparted in these institutions had not diffused Knowledge among the masses. The Munroe Enquiry, however, resulted in the Establishment of Collectorate and Tahsildary Schools in each district.[2]

Missionary Activities

Thanks to the efforts of Jesuit Missionary with its headquarters at Tiruchirappalli, schools sprang up at various places in rapid succession in the second half of the nineteenth century and they proved to be very popular. Most important of such schools came to be the English and Tamil schools founded by the famous Missionary Schwartz.[3]

A Collectorate and many Tahsildary Schools came to be organized in the district region as a sequel to the efforts of the Board of Instruction set up, as a result of the Munroe enquiry. But owing to the mode of selection, the low pay, the absence of stimulus to the teacher, the want of all training and the entire absence of supervision, the new scheme was a total failure. Meanwhile the Anglo-vernacular controversy was set in motion and the Committee of Native Education replaced the Board of Instruction. This new body introduced the Normal School and Taluk School Scheme. Of these, the former was meant for the training of teacher while the latter taught vernacular, English and other modern subjects. These developments led to a considerable progress in the field of education in the district, which was further strengthened by the Local Funds and Town Improvement Acts of 1871. As a consequence of these and the rapid rise in philanthropic activities, the census of 1901 recorded that 13 per cent of the female were literates. The census data on literacy further reveals that the percentage of literacy was higher in regions of concentrated missionary activities.[4]

Thus Tiruchirappalli and Karur taluks recorded comparatively higher literacy percentage. At the opening of twentieth century, the district had 6 Upper Secondary, 28 Lower Secondary, 2 Training Schools And two Colleges. Apart from these a few Technical Institutions also existed in the district. Tiruchirappalli taluk had one Upper Secondary and 18 Lower Secondary Schools along with 3 Training Schools.[5]

Elementary Education

Until 1920, Elementary Education was left in the hands of private individuals and Local Bodies. But in 1920, when the Elementary Education Act was enacted, there was an Educational Council set up for each district consisting of persons, some nominated by the Government and other selected by the Local Bodies. All matters concerning education were dealt with in consultation with this body. The Council was established in Tiruchirappalli and it laid great emphasis on wide diffusion of Elementary Education. The Madras Education Act was later modified so as to introduce an element of compulsion. This empowered the heads of Municipalities, District Boards, etc., to impose penalties on parents who withdrew their children from Elementary Schools. The District Educational Councils established in 1939, were in turn abolished in 1941, and their powers were vested to the Department of Education.[6]

In 1946, the element of compulsion and penal power, which vested with the Municipal Chairman, President, District Board etc., was transferred to the District Educational Officers. The overall effect of these measures was to raise the percentage of pupil studying in V standard to total admissions considerably.[7]

As a consequence of various measures adopted by the Government, Elementary Education has progressed very much in the district. But the fact remains that much more has to be achieved. At the opening of the 1951, there were 1,496 primary Schools in the district and as many as 134 of these institutions were run by the Government. The strength of number of institutions increased from 2056 in 1930-31 to 2519 in 1959-60.[8]

The total strength of the students in Elementary schools was 1,57,597 in 1950-51. The number of institutions as well as pupils increased rapidly during the decade 1959-60. The number of pupils had increased to 2,49,900.[9]

Secondary Education

The two enactments of 1871 acted as a great stimulant to the growth of Secondary Education in the district. The formation of a number of Local Boards and Municipalities led to the opening of a number of educational institutions of this category. The Local Funds and Town Improvements Act of 1871 entrusted education to the Local bodies which made sincere efforts towards making education available to the public.[10] The effects of these measures were soon begun to be felt and the opening of the twentieth century witnessed marked advance in the field of secondary Education in the district.

There was one Government school in Trichinopoly, intended especially for Mohammedans. It was started in 1873, and is located in a room over the Post Office in the building attached to the main guard gate in the fort. On the 31st march 1875 there were 73 boys in this school and 65 on the 31st march 1876. Its cost is defrayed from provincial funds, the charge on which on account of it for 1875-76 was rupee 454-11-6. Tamil, Hindustani and English were taught in this school which has been on the whole successful so far, and has, in all probability, had the effect of creating a desire among the Musalman population for education.[11]

During the last few decades, the Tiruchirappalli district in common with other districts experienced far-reaching changes in the field of Secondary Education. Secondary Education ended with Matriculation Examination conducted by the University. In 1911, it was replaced by the Secondary School Leaving Certificate Examination conducted by the Board of Secondary Education. In 1925, the managers of private schools were given freedom to choose the medium of instruction.[12] Though these measures resulted in the progress of Secondary Education, much had remained to be done then. The tables shown in the reference-12 show the progress made in the number of institutions and in the number of pupils during the last few decades.

The introduction of Basic Education had given a new orientation to Elementary Education. The main purpose of this scheme is to terminate the system of learning solely from books and give the children a change to develop the initiative, enterprise and resourcefulness in them. Children were taught basic crafts like spinning, weaving etc., so as to make productive work, the basis of any learning. The aim of the Government was to convert all the existing Elementary Schools into Basic Schools and provide at least one Basic School for all villages with a population above 500. During 1959-60, there were 200 basic Schools in the district with 35,200 pupils attending them.[13]

With a view to give a new look to Secondary Education a revised curriculum was drawn up in 1948. This was prepared in consultation with experienced teachers, of the public and the Board of Secondary Education. The main features of this scheme were the introduction of Basic Craft as a part of the school curriculum and the integration of History, Geography and Civics in to one subject under the head Social Studies. All other subject retained their respective places.

In giving an account of the system of education pursued in the Trichinopoly district, the best course seems to be to follow the classification of schools adopted by the Educational Department. There was no institution in the district up to B.A standard, but the S.P.G. (Society for Propagation of the Gospel) High school in Trichinopoly taught up to the level of First Arts. This school was one of the most important of the aided collegiate schools and one of the largest educational institutions in the Presidency. There were 664 pupils in the school on the 31st March, 1874, 702 on the 31st March, 1875 and 783 on the 31st March, 1876. Of those receiving instruction on the later date, 30 were in the collegiate, 186 in the Higher and 389 in the Lower department.[14] From the above said facts and figures we could conclude that there was an over all and gradual growth in the educational condition of the District and a momentum had gathered for the further development.

Roman Catholic Missionaries conducted most of the institutions. There is also a school for girls in Trichinopoly known as Lady Hobart's Girls' School. It was opened in 1874 and is held in a portion of the Nawab's palace, the strength of Mohammedan girl's not correctly known, but total strength as on 31st March 1876 was 59.[15]

The degree of education in Tiruchinopoly is rather above the average for the whole Presidency, but below that for the Southern districts. At the census of 1901, thirteen percent of the male population of the old district and eight in every thousand of the women and girls could read and write, while the corresponding figures for the Presidency as a whole were 12 and 9 and for the Southern districts 14 and 9.[16]

As was to be expected a good deal of differences occurs in the degree of literacy attained in the different parts of the district. Far ahead of all others comes the head quarter Taluk, in which 23 per cent of the male and 21 per cent of the females can read and write; it is followed after a long interval by Karur in which the corresponding figures are 10 and 6; and the most backward of all the taluks is Perambalur, where they are 8 and 2 respectively.[17]

Of the members of the three leading religions, the Mohammedans were far ahead of the others in the matter of male education, while in the education of their women the Christians equally outstripped the others. The Hindus come last in both cases. The percentages of the males who could read and write in 1901 were 11 among Hindus, 27 among Mohammedans and 16 among Christians; while the corresponding figures per thousand of the other sex were 5, 15 and 48.[18] The Mohammedans are a trading community to whom knowledge of reading and writing is essential. The Christians benefit from the efforts of the missionaries being best educated where missionary enterprise is keenest. In Karur Taluk no less than 37 per cent males and 25 per cent of the females can read and write.[19]

At the close of the year 1905, the higher educational institutions of the district included six secondary and 28 lower secondary schools, three training schools and the District Board's sectional schools, six Technical and industrial schools, and two colleges namely St. Josephs and S.P.G College in Trichinopoly town.[20]

There are six upper secondary schools situated in Tiruchinopoly, Srirangam, Lalgudi, Kattuputtur, Karur and Naamakkal. Of the 28 Lower secondary schools 18 are situated in Trichinopoly taluk and the rest 10 in Trichinopoly town.[21]

The 3 training schools are at work in Trichinopoly town. One of them is a Government institution for masters, and the two are for school mistresses and are managed by missionary bodies. The District Board's Sessional school has been established for the Training and education of primary school masters in rural tracts. The teachers receive a meager stipend while under instruction.[22]

The St. Josephs College at Trichinopoly is the first grade institution and the second one is S.P.G College founded by Schwartz in 1766 as 'an English and a Tamil school' and maintained it out of his own salary.[23]

The college had established with 202 students. Mohammedans are in every case charged half rates. The charges for boarding were Rs. 7-8 for a month for Brahmins and Rs. 2 for Christians. Mohammedans paid half of rate of Brahmins.[24]

Collegiate Education

In the field of Collegiate Education, private agencies and individuals have also played a prominent role. The Jesuit Mission had started a College at Nagapattinam in Thanjavur district in 1840. But soon it was realized that Nagapattinam was not a suitable place to establish a College. Hence, in 1883 the College was shifted to Tiruchirappalli. Thus, the St. Joseph's College was shifted to Tiruchirappalli. Due to want of accommodation, the College was first housed in the 'Clive House.' The building for the College was opened in 1885 only. Elaborate arrangements have been made for the accommodation of students both the Christians and the non-Christians.[25] This institution has grown to the status of the premier collegiate institution in the district and rank among the leading institutions of its kind in the state.

The next important institution that started functioning in Tiruchirappalli was the S.P.G College, run by the Society for the Propagation of Gospel. This college was the result of the upgrading of the Tamil-English School, established by the famous Missionary Schwartz in 1766. After a century and more this school in Tiruchirappalli was raised to the status of a Second Grade College in 1873 and later it became a first grade college affiliated to the Madras University.[26] But during early days of the present century, this college had to be closed and the institution now functions only as a High School.

However, due to the interest shown by private agencies remarkable progress was achieved in this field. At the close of 1955 A.D there were six colleges in the district. They were the St. Joseph's College, the National College, the Jamal Mohamed College, the Holy Cross College, the Sitalakshmi Ramaswamy College and the Rajah's College at Pudukkottai. All the institutions were the outcome of philanthropic moves and recently the government had taken over the Rajah's College at Pudukkottai subsequently.

The number of students in these colleges has recorded considerable increase since 1951. During this year, there were 3,174 students studying in these colleges. Their number had increased to 5,003 during 1960-61. The number of teaching staff had also recorded a satisfactory increase during the decade.[27]

Besides these regular colleges, there are two Training Colleges in the district *viz.*, the Government Training College at Pudukkottai and Vivekanada Training College, run by the Ramakrishna Mission at Tiruparayturai. Together these two institutions had 143 students on their rolls during 1960-61.[28]

In Tiruchirappalli District, 24 per cent of male and 39 per cent of female in the Muslim community are illiterate. 34 per cent of male and 44 per cent of female studied up to eighth standard, 15 per cent of male and 10 per cent of female studied up to tenth standard, 10 percent of male and 5 per cent of female studied up to twelfth standard, 10 per cent of male and 2 per cent of female are graduates, 2 to 3 per cent male are post-graduates, less than 1 per cent of female are post-graduates.[29] The above mentioned statistical points are related to 1991 census of India.

The following Muslim educational institutions of Tiruchirappalli District were established by the efforts of the Muslim philanthropists: Jamal Mohammed College, Trichy Town, M.I.E.T Arts and Science College, Trichy Town, M.I.E.T Engineering College, Trichy Town, M.I.E.T Polytechnic, Trichy Town, A.I.M.A.N Arts and Science College for women, Trichy Town, Khaja Mian Higher Secondary School. Trichy Town, Khaja Mian Polytechnic, Trichy Town, Abdul Samad High School, (CBSE Syllabus), Trichy Town, Hajrath Syed Murthuza Higher Secondary School, Palakarai, Trichy, Viscountes Corshan Muslim Girl's School, Trichy Town, Uswathun Hasana Oriental Arabic Girl's Higher Secondary School, Pallapatti, Uswathun Hasana Oriental Arabic Boy's Higher Secondary School, Pallapatti, Quaide Millath Higher Elementary School, Pallapatti, Muidul Islam School, Chinna

Darapuram, Karur and Moulana Higher Secondary School, Perambalur.

Muslim Educational Institutions in Tiruchirappalli

There are many century old centres for learning Muslim religious education in Tiruchirappalli district. But for western education we could see no institutions before 1915. To our great surprise, the first school started for the Muslims was a school for girls. In 1917, the Viceroy Lord Viscountes Corshan started a school for the Muslim girls.[30] Syed Murthuza Sahib established an institution in 1887 named as Madrasa-i-Shamshia, an elementary school which later converted into a high school and handed it over to the Government in 1919.[31] The Government then named that school after his name. Now it is flourishing as Syed Murthuza Government Higher Secondary School located at Palakarai. At present, 1500 pupils are studying in the school; among that 60 per cent are Muslims.

Syed Murthuza was born in 1863. He was a great freedom fighter and potential member of the Indian National Congress. His forefathers migrated from Bukhara (Russia) to India. He studied up to F.A. He went to Aligarh and joined Sir Syed Ahmed Khan in his intellectual Aligarh movement. He returned to Tiruchirappalli and involved himself in awakening the Muslims towards the freedom struggle and Western learning. He was appointed as the Law council member in the year 1912 went to Delhi and received the 'Right Honourable' title from the British Government. But such titles never set him apart from the freedom struggle. He was an active participant in the Khilafat Movement in 1919.[32] Apart from his participation in the freedom movement his services to the cause of education of the Muslim is a noteworthy one.

Syed Murthuza, a pioneer of the cause of the education of the Muslims, has set himself as an example for others to follow. He was the first to start a Muslim Elementary school in the Trichy District which in due course developed as a Higher Secondary school which was named after him by the Government. He was selected by the Congress party as a

Member of Legislative Assembly in 1921. He raised his voice for the cause of the education of the Muslims in the Assembly many a time. He was sent to Delhi in 1928 to study and analyse the Nehru Report.[33] Till his death he worked for the betterment of the Muslims' socio-economic conditions.

Another Muslim Philanthropist of Trichy district was Haji. M.N. Khajamiah Rowther. Haji Khajamian Sahib born in 1880 started his career as a humble businessman and later involved himself in Leather Tannery Industry. He became an expert in that business and became a Technocrat of Leather Technology. He acquired wealth in due course and spent his wealth for the development of Muslim religious education as well as for Western education. Thus, he was successful in making both the ends meet. He was a staunch freedom fighter and a Member of Indian National Congress. He wore 'Kader' as advocated by Gandhiji and started a 'Kader Industry.' He gave 120 acres of land for the establishment of Jamal Mohammed College. He showed his philanthropic altruism to the religious education of the Muslims by establishing 'Jamia Anwarul Ulum Arabic College' in 1914. He also sympathized with the orphans which resulted in the construction of an orphanage near the Arabic College. A High school was established in 1962 after the name of Haji Khaja Mian Sahib. At present it is flourishing as Higher Secondary School with more than 4000 students.[34]

Jamal Mohammed College, Tiruchirappalli

Next to the above-mentioned educational institutions, an institution, dedicated to the cause of Muslim education is the Jamal Mohamed College. It was the first institution for Higher education established by the Muslims in Tiruchirappalli District. The beginning was no doubt humble. In terms of building, the College had only the main block, which was used to house laboratories and library. Classes were conducted only in the thatched sheds. Godowns for salted-hides were used as hostels.

The Colleges offering Graduate and postgraduate courses to the aspiring students were a few and far as under in the early years of 1950s. Besides, majority of these institutions had been managed by particular sections in the society who had already been considered educationally advanced. They had been giving preference, naturally, in the matter of admission to those students who belonged to their own communities. Students belonging to a substantial section of the society, especially Muslims, who just then had started showing some interest in acquiring collegiate education, could not readily get admission in these institutions. This was the time when Jamal Mohamed College made its appearance on the map of higher education in India as "a rising star in the firmament of academic horizon."

The relevance of this college, however, came soon to be recognized and its service to the society gained wide appreciation. The College Management's resolute decision, not to collect any money in the name of 'Capitation fee' or at the time of admission helped thousand of students especially poor Muslim youth to gain higher studies in this college. This fact greatly added to the reputation of the college. As a result a good number of philanthropists volunteered to undertake the construction of new structures.

The college was established in 1951 by the philanthropic magnanimity of N.M. Khajamian Rowther and M.J. Jamal Mohamed Rowther. Haji Khajamian Sahib donated 120 acres of land for starting the college. The college was built by Haji Jamal Mohamed Sahib. The Jamal Mohamed College was established in the year 1951 at Tiruchirappalli. The founders of this college are Janab Khajamian and Janab M.J Jamal Mohamed of revered memory. The College stands as an eternal testimony to the enormity of wisdom, farsightedness and philanthropic gesture of these two noble founders. The American Stanford Foundation had chosen 20 colleges from India as the best to receive aid from it. Jamal Mohammed College was one among the 20 colleges, chosen by the foundation to receive its aid. It attracts students not only from all over India, but also from foreign countries like Malaysia, Singapore, Thailand and Fuji islands.[35]

Haji Jamal Mohamed was born in the year 1881. His father Haji Jamal Mohideen from Ramanathapuram visited Madras for a business purpose and later settled there. Haji Jamal Mohamed learnt English and Tamil in the Christian College, Madras. He indulged himself in Leather Tanning business and with his inborn talent he became a very successful businessman.

Before the First World War he visited Europe on a business tour. There he had a princely chance of meeting the Great Ministers and Politicians. Similarly, he travelled to Turkey and met many officials of 'Anjuman-i-Ithihatheqaum, a famous institution in Turkey. He also met the leaders of Egypt's Freedom Movement. The tour he made to Europe and to the Muslim countries benefited him in many ways especially in his business.[36]

Haji Jamal Mohamed took useful measures to add Modern educational subjects and English along with the Madarsa education. But he was cautious that the Madrasa education should not lose its importance. As an initiative, he selected scholars from all over India and appointed them in his Madrasa. This brought a dramatic change in the development of the education of the Muslim students. His business also developed well as the years passed. His dedication to the development of Muslim education is incomparable. He started a boarding house for the welfare of the poor students. This enabled many poor students to continue their education staying in that boarding house. About 100-150 students were benefited. The students of the hostel were also provided with bus fare every month. The boarding house was successfully run for the next four years. Many students studied there and later settled in their lives in various fields.

Haji Jamal Mohamed planned to conduct five seminars a year for the benefit of the students in his institution. For that he spent about Rs. 3,000 and invited scholars from all over India. An association was formed with the leadership of the South Indian Association of Muslim Educational Institutions. The first seminar was about the life of Prophet Mohamed

(Pbuh) by Allama Mohammed Iqbal. His elegant speech was appreciated by everyone. Later that speech was published as a book by a publishing company named 'Dharul Musanni Bin Writers House' with the name 'Khudh Bathe Madras'. The book brought a dramatic change in the lives of many youngsters. The next year a scholar named Maarma Duke Bikthal delivered his speech on the 'Cultural scope of the Muslims'. This speech was also published as a book in English, later. In the third year Sir Mohamed Iqbal gave seminar on the topic 'The importance of Islam'. His speeches were of great value that it was published every time. His speech focussed on many angles emphasizing on the importance of Islam.[37]

Haji Jamal Mohamed not only rendered his service to the Muslims in Tamilnadu, but also thought for the benefit of the Muslim institutions in other parts of India. The Vice-Chancellor of Jamia Milliyah (a popular educational institution in Delhi), Zahir Hussain (former President of India) asked Mazihil Mulk Hakim Ajmal Khan, his subordinate to go to Madras and collect funds from the Muslim philanthropist because Jamia Milliyah had a great downfall in its progress. But, on the way to Chennai, Hakim Ajmal Khan died, so Dr. Zahir Hussain, the Vice-Chancellor himself met Jamal Mohamed sahib and explained about the pathetic condition of the Jamia Milliyah. Within a short time Haji Jamal Mohamed Sahib collected Rs. 75,000 and handed over to Zahir Hussain. He did not stop with it. Later he collected Rs. 40,000 from the Muslim businessmen in Madras and sent it to Jamia Milliyah. Thus he gave a revival to Jamia Milliyah.[38]

Jamal Mohamed was not only an educationalist but also an economic expert. He criticized the British government when it reduced the value of Indian rupee. He wrote many articles and essays on this, which was published in leading newspapers. On seeing his writings in the newspapers the Madras University invited him for the first time in the history of it, a non-graduate to deliver a speech on the economy of the country. Later it selected him as one of the members of the council of Commerce. He did not spare the political field also. He was chosen by the British Government of India to take part in the First Round Table Conference held in London in the year 1930. After, his return from England he paid his attention to reform Arabic Madrasas. In 1945 the Tannery industries had a great setback. Haji Jamal Mohammed's business also declined. Even then he never gave up his heart; with great difficulties he repaid all his debts. This proved his honesty in the business field.[39]

Haji Jamal Mohammed had a proposal to start a college for the Muslim community in Tiruchirappalli. The need for more Muslim colleges and the sad plight of the Muslim students who aspired in vain for higher education had been agitating the mind of Haji Jamal Mohammed. The late Janab N.M.Khajamian Rowther and the late Janab M. Jamal Mohamed Sahib planned to meet this challenge by establishing a First Grade College in Tiruchirappalli, considered being the heart of Tamilnadu. Jamal Mohamed College made its appearance thus in the map of academic world on 11th July 1951. The college was inaugurated by Hon.P.S.Kumarasamy Raja, the Chief Minister of Madras, when His Excellency, the Maharaja of Bhavanagar, the then Governor of Madras, very graciously presided.

Jamal Mohamed College has been growing in strength and stature ever since its inception. The 'JAMAL' now is a household name in Tamilnadu and foreign countries where people of Indian origin live in sizable numbers. The college has now come to symbolize the fulfillment of the long-felt needs and cherished aspirations of millions of people living in these places, especially the Muslim community.

When the college was inaugurated it had only two courses to offer, about 200 students on the roll and around 20 members on the staff. There was just a single building, the magnificent Main Block with only ground floor to house the laboratories and the libraries. The institution, however, was destined to grow and there has been a phenomenal growth and expansion in the sprawling campus of over 100 acres donated by the late Alhaj N.M. Khajamian Rowther. The number of courses offered at the Under-graduate level kept on increasing .A grand Mosque, a spacious Auditorium, several imposing structures for hostel, classes and library were started to adorn the landscape of Jamal. The enormous growth registered by the college within a short span of time was so much prolific and impressive.

The year 1963-64 is a landmark in the history of Jamal for it witnessed the inauguration of two Post-Graduate Courses in Mathematics and Economics. Dr. Zakir Hussain, then Vice-President of the Republic of India, was the chief guest of honour on the occasion of the inaugural function.[40] Since then it grew in quality and quantity thus, the college, now offers 13 UG courses and 15 PG courses, 5 Diploma courses, and M.Phil, and Research programmers in six Departments.

Exclusive Section for Girls

The Academic year 1999-2000 marked another importance in the history of the college. The doors of the colleges were thrown open to the girl students. Three exclusive sections were started for the girls and in the current year two more sections are added. There was overwhelming response from the public to the step taken by the management, to extend the facilities available to the girl students who also aspire for higher education. The strength of the college has grown from mere 200 in 1951 to 3800 in 2000, out of which 400 are women students.

The college has two hostels, one is paid and the other one is called "Mosque Hostel" run free for the poor Muslim students. Many dignitaries who have adorned the seats of highest offices visited the college and delivered speeches.[41]

Education in Thanjavur District

Prior to the establishment of British rule its early days of education was left to the local initiative. Only after the first half of the nineteenth Century the State began making attempts to encourage education. The position of education in the district during the close of the first quarter of the last century was indeed much disheartening. Public instruction was not considered as the duty of the state, even though the local Chieftains sometimes took pains to patronize it.

The State-wide enquiry conducted by Sir Thomas Munroe in 1822 revealed the existence of several schools and colleges in the district. These schools were pyall schools to teach the young to write, read and recite, while the colleges were mostly Vedapatasalas attended generally by Brahmin boys who were taught the sciences of Grammar, Logic and Literature. The enquiry further revealed that the district had 109 colleges and 884 schools with about 769 and 17,582 pupils respectively. But due to the peculiar nature of instruction imparted in these institutions, the diffusion of knowledge among the masses was next to nothing. The Munroe Enquiry however resulted in the establishment of a collectorate and Thasildari schools in each district.[42]

The Christian Missionaries in the district took keen interest in the spread of education. The role of the Lutheran Mission, Wesleyan Mission and Roman Catholic Mission is commendable. The enquiry of 1822 revealed the existence of 19 Missionary schools in the district and their number had risen to 33 by 1870.[43]

As a result of the Munroe Enquiry, a collectorate school and a few Thasildari schools came to be organized in the district. Of these the Collectorate School was at Nagapattinam and the Thasildari schools were set up at Thiruvarur, Kumbakonam, Thiruvaiyar and Mannargudi. But owing to the mode of selection, low pay, absence of stimulus in the teachers, want of training and the entire absence of supervision, the new scheme was a total failure. Meanwhile the Anglo-vernacular controversy was set in motion and the Board of Instruction was replaced by the Committee of Native Education. This body introduced the Normal School Scheme. The committee set up a Normal school at Mayuram and Taluk schools at Thiruvaiyar, Thiruvarur, Tiruvidaimarudur, Pattukottai and Nagore. Of these the former was meant for the training of teachers while the latter taught local language, English and other subjects to children. After this landmark there was considerable progress in the field of education in the district which was further strengthened by the Local Funds and Town Improvement Act of 1871. On the eve of the enactments of 1871 the district had 58 aided schools of which 14 were meant for girls.[44]

At the dawn of the nineteenth century education in Tanjore district was almost entirely imparted in the indigenous institutions. Except a few missionary schools, most of the schools and higher institutions of learning, which may be called as colleges were supported either by the funds provided by Raja Sarabhoji or by the contributions, paid by the students. In 1823, for instance, it was found that there were 884 schools and 109 colleges in the district. At the close of the nineteenth century, there were 41 free schools, 19 run by Christian missionaries, 21 by the Raja, and 1 by the Thiruvarur temple and none by any Muslim for Muslims. These schools taught reading writing and arithmetic normally for a period of 5 years to the pupils of all castes of the Hindus as well as to those of the Muslims and Christians. For example in a school there were 128 Brahmins students, 34 other caste Hindus, only one Harijan and 30 Christians but no Muslim students![45]

The educational scenario in the beginning of the twentieth century was quite interesting. The people of Tanjore were exceptionally well educated according to the statistics of the census of 1901. The district comes first in the literacy of its total population in the Presidency. In female education rate the district is backward, standing only at seventh place. About ten persons in every 100 can read and write, and among the male population the number rises to 20 in every hundred.[46]

Education is particularly advanced in the largest municipalities. The towns of Tanjore, Kumbakonam, and Mannargudi stand first and second respectively, in general education of all the towns in the Presidency, passing even Madras, and if male education be considered, the third place is taken by Nagapatnam the result is largely due to the wealth, as well as to the natural intelligence, of the people of the district; but another cause is to be found in the high degree of education, comparatively attained by the Mohammedans and it is this which raises Tanjore in point of literacy above Malabar, where education among Hindus is more widely spread.[47]

The adherents of the three chief religions in the beginning of the twentieth century are about equally literate: of the Hindus about 10 per cent can read and write and of the Mohammedans and Christians about 11 per cent. As might be expected, the great majority of the literate persons have been educated in Tamil. Eight persons in every thousand are able to write English and in this respect also Tanjore stands high among the districts of the presidency. Among the various taluks, Nagapatnam (probably owing to the large number of Lebbais included in its population) contains the highest proportion of educated persons, and Pudukkottai the smallest. Tanjore, Kumbakonam, Mayavaram and Mannargudi are also advanced, while Tirutturaippundi is backward.[48]

It is also a striking fact that in various colleges in Madras and Trichinopoly many more students come from Tanjore than from any other district. In 1906, there were 11 first grade Colleges in Madras Presidency among them two belong to this (Tanjore) district.[49]

Elementary Education

Until 1920 elementary education was left in the hands of private agencies like missionaries, private individuals and local bodies. The state did not interfere at all. But in 1920 the Elementary Education Act was enacted which set up an education council for each district in the state consisting of persons, some nominated by the Government and other elected by the local bodies. All matters concerning elementary education were decided by consulting this body. This council was established in Thanjavur also. This council laid great emphasis on wide diffusion of Elementary Education. The

Madras education act of 1920 was later modified so as to introduce an element of compulsion. This empowered the heads of Municipalities, District Boards etc., to impose penalties on parents who withdrew their children from elementary schools. The District Education council was replaced by the Taluk Advisory Council in 1939, which was in turn abolished in 1941 after which their powers were vested to the Department of Education.[50]

In 1946 the element of compulsion and penal power, which vested with the Municipal Chairman, President, District Board etc., was transferred to the District Educational Officers. The overall effect of these measures was to raise the percentage of pupils studying in 5th Standard to total admissions considerably.[51]

As a consequence of various measure adopted by the Government, Elementary education has progressed very much in the district. But the fact remains that much more has to be achieved. The analysis of the data as given in the tables shown in the reference will give an idea of the general trend of progress recorded in elementary education during the last few decades in the district.[52] There was a decrease in the number of institutions of the Government.

Secondary Education

The enactments of 1871 acted as a great stimulant to the growth of Secondary education in the district. The formation of a number of Local Boards and Municipalities led to the opening of a number of educational institutions of this category. The Local Funds and Town Improvement Act of 1871 entrusted education to the local bodies, which made sincere efforts for making education available to the pupil.[53]The efforts of these measures began to be felt soon and the dawn of the twentieth century witnessed marked advance in the field of Secondary education in Thanjavur district.

During the last few decades the district in common with other districts experienced far reaching change in the field of secondary education. Secondary education hitherto ended with Matriculation Examination conducted by the university. In 1911 it was replaced by the S.S.L.C. Examination conducted by the Board of Secondary education. In 1925 the managers of private schools were given freedom to choose the medium of instruction.[54] Though these measures resulted in the progress of Secondary education much remained to be done. The two tables given in the reference show the progress made in the number of institution and in the number of pupils respectively during the last few decades.

As in the case of Tiruchirappalli district, in Thanjavur district too a new orientation has been given to Elementary education by the introduction of Basic Education. It gave the children a chance to develop the initiative, to pursue the knowledge that is more practical, and to nurture the resourcefulness in every child. Children are taught basic crafts like spinning, weaving etc., so as to make productive work the basis of learning. The Government aimed to convert all the existing elementary schools into basic schools and provide at least one basic school for all villages with a population of over 500 persons. During 1959-60, there were 408 basic schools with over 61,000 pupils.[55]

With a view to give a new look to Secondary education, a revised curriculum was drawn up in 1948. This was prepared in consultation with experienced teachers, the public and the Board of secondary Education. The main features of this scheme were the introduction of basic craft as a part of the school curriculum and the integration of History, Geography and Civics into one subject under the head 'Social Studies'. All other subjects retained their respective places.

Collegiate Education

In the field of collegiate education private agencies also have played a prominent role in the district. The first college to be established in the district was the Kumbakonam College, which was formed by upgrading the school there. This college was started as a second grade college in 1864 and four years later it was made a first grade college getting affiliated to the Madras University. Following this two other schools were upgraded and made into colleges early during twentieth century. Thus in 1905, the St. Peter's College and Findley's College were opened at Thanjavur and Mannargudi respectively.[56] But these colleges did not last long. Hence the Kumbakonam College was the only collegiate institution in Thanjavur for a long time. The strength of this Government managed institution, increased regularly so as to meet the requirements of the district.

However, during early second half of this century i.e. during the last decade, four more colleges were opened in Thanjavur. They are the A.V.C College, Mayuram; the Khadir Mohideen College, Adirampattinam; Raja Serfoji College, Thanjavur and the Sri Pushpam College at Poondi. Though these colleges are under Private Managements they have recorded good progress since their inception. These colleges for a long time did not admit girl students, however now they began to enrolling them.

Apart from these regular colleges, there exists a training college at Orathanad. This college trains teachers for the Basic schools and 328 students attended the training course during 1960-61. Thanjavur is rich in oriental college and these are four colleges of oriented learning. They are Karanthai Pulavar Kolloori, the Oriental College at Dharmapuram, Raja's College of Sanskrit and Tamil studies and the Srilashri Kasivasi Swaminatha Swamigal Senthamil Kalloori at Tiruppanandal. Detailed statistics of pupils and teaching staff have been furnished separately.

In the words of Henry George, "Education continues to be the principal hope promoting progress. The success of most progressive ideas, embodying every phase of life, depends upon an intelligent citizen's body to make them practicable. Lack of understanding on the part of the people had ruined the change of success of many splendid plans."

Adirampattinam is a small town situated on the South-East coast of the Bay of Bengal. It occupies a significant place in Tanjore District in catering to the educational service to their inhabitants and improving their intellectual capacity. Adirampattinam took a lead position in promoting the cause of education of this long East coast region people in general and the Muslims in particular. Even though there were many rich people in this coastal line and nearby Pattukottai, only Adirampattinam Maraikkayars took initiative to establish schools and colleges. This achievement of pride and administration is the result of the work of a Muslim Philanthropist, Haji M.K.N. Khadir Mohideen Maraikar and his brothers.

The Arabic oriental schools and Madrasas are the oldest institutions in this place. These schools offer facilities to pupil to acquire the rudiments of Knowledge in Arabic language. There are three oriental residential schools here. Students from far and near come to these schools. For religious, charitable, educational and other noble purposes, Adirampattinam was never found want of funding. M.K.N. Khadir Mohideen, the greatest philanthropist of Adirampattinam, made a princely donation of all his wealth, 1255 acres of land, for the lighting and maintenance of Mosques and promotion of Arabic learning, Islamic studies and the religious interest of the community. His equally liberal hearted brothers M.K.N. Ahamed Thambi, M.K.N. Naina Mohammed Lebbai and M.K.N. Shaik Lebbai willingly contributed their quota of 210 acres of land. Together they created the M.K.N Madrasa on 16-12-1900, the benefaction comprising, thus, 1465 acres of land, whose present Capital value exceeds in crores. The oldest Madrasa in Adirampattinam was started by this trust namely Madrasa Salahiya founded in the year 1900. This Madrasa offering free meals and accommodation to all the scholars who join Madrasa for religious learning.[57] It also offers financial assistance towards the boarding expenses of 15 scholars and salary of two teachers of Rahmania Madrasa which is another sister institution founded in 1926 in Adirampattinam.[58] Khadir Mohideen was the donor of Bikhu Malai; composed by poet

Khadir Mohideen Annaviar (Bikhu Malai is being reprinted with the financial assistance of A.J. Iqbal Hajiyar and A.M. Shamsuddin Hajiyar).

In the month of Ramzan, people from several places would throng in large number to meet Khadir Mohideen Maraikkar and receive Zakath (religious charity). Apart from this he would also distribute charity (Sathaqua) cheerfully, true to the saying "Great Charity is, that which is offered by the right hand without the knowledge of the left hand". To the poor parents who could not afford to give their daughters in Marriage he would offer monetary and material assistance and provide married life for those girls. M.M. Mohamed Dhaha, a poet of Adirampattinam, glorifies the philanthropy of the 'Vallal' as *'Athiyaman of Adirampattinam'* and as *'Adirai Eeentha Arumkodai Vallal.'* (The great Philanthropist of Adirampattinam).[59]

The first step towards the dissemination of education on Western lines in the region was taken by the Muslim minority. The state Government also supported rich Muslims to start Educational Institutions by giving financial aids. The Government also took equal interest in opening many Panchayath Elementary schools here. The educational expansion received full impetus in this area only after the attainment of Independence. Compulsory education was introduced in primary schools and to feed the poor school-going children, many Muslims contributed their mite and helped the plan to run successfully.

The control of education is placed under the Chief Educational Officer at district level. The chief Educational Officer is assisted by District Educational Officer. The District Educational Officer is assisted by the Deputy Inspector of Schools. There are four types of schools namely, Primary schools, Higher Elementary schools, High schools and Higher Secondary schools. Further there are two types of colleges, Professional Colleges and Arts Colleges.

As the result of Government's policy of secularism and the minority rights given to the minority religious communities, the following educational institutions have been established by philanthropic efforts of the Muslims of Thanjavur district: Kasimiah Higher Secondary School, Rajagiri (1948), Khadir Mohideen Higher Secondary School, Adirampattinam (1949), Sarekath Islam Higher Secondary School, Valuthur (1961), Crescent Higher Secondary School, Avaniyapuram (1971) and Khadir Mohideen Girl's Higher Secondary School, Adirampattinam (1989). Apart from this Government aided schools there are five Matriculation Higher Secondary Schools and twelve Matriculation Schools conducted by the Muslim people. The starting of Khadir Mohideen College in Adirampattinam in 1955 is a landmark in the educational history of Thanjavur district.

Among the Muslim centres in Thanjavur district, Adirampattinam has a unique place in the educational map. There are Five Panchayath Primary School, Two Panchayath Higher Elementary Schools, One Panchayath girls High School, One Khadir Mohideen Girls Higher secondary School, Onc Khadir Mohideen higher Secondary School, One Imam Shafi Matric and Higher Secondary School, One Khadir Mohideen College and One Saduliya Industrial Training Institute.

History of Khadir Mohideen College Adirampattinam

The need for more colleges and the said plight of students who aspired in vain for higher education had been agitating the minds of many educationists. Members of the leading and noble Maraikar family shared this anxiety and planned to meet this challenge. The high-minded Philanthropist Haji M.K.N. Khadir Mohideen Maraikkar after whom the college has been named and the equally large hearted three brothers of him namely, Janab M.K.N. Naina Mohamed Lebbai Maraikar, Janab M.K.N. Ahamed Thambi Maraikar, Haji M.K.N. Shaik Salath Lebbai Maraikar decided to establish a second grade College; and a Committee was formed to work for its establishment. Further, it donated the vast exclusive lands to the proposed college.[60] However the starting of the college was not given immediate effect.

The board of trustees under the chairmanship of S.M.S. Shaik Jalaludeen, a grand son of the great donors who assumed the charge of the M.K.N. Madrasa trust, approached the University of Madras for its recognition and affiliation. The recognition was granted by the great and illustrious educationist, Dr. A. Lakshmanaswami Mudaliar, the then vice Chancellor of the Madras University. The College was formerly declared open by the Honourable Thiru C. Subramaniam, the Education Minister of Madras in 1955.[61]

Haji S.M.S.Sheik Jalaludeen, a great visionary with his farsighted vision converted the M.K.N. Madrasa into an instrument of cataclysmic change in secular education, in addition to looking after the religious interests of the community in accordance with the wishes of the donors. Because of his Herculean efforts, the M.K.N. Madrasa gave birth to Khadir Mohideen High School in 1949, college in 1955, higher secondary school in 1978, Girls High School in 1982. Sadulia Nursery School was started as allied institution and placed in charge of his son S. Mohamed Mohideen. A Mosque was constructed inside the college campus. He conceived the plan of starting 'one Post Graduate course every year' and elevated the status of the college as a premier Post-Graduate institution by launching M.Com., in 1985 and M.Sc., Chemistry in 1986. Rightly, S.M.S. Shaik Jalaludeen is hailed as *Kalvithanthai*, good father of education of Adirampattinam.

S.M.S. Shaik Jalaludeen's mantle fell on the shoulders of his son S. Mohamed Mohideen who implemented the scheme of his father with great vigour. Every year U.G or P.G courses like B.B.A., B.Sc., Computer science, M.Sc., Zoology were added. He elevated the status of the college still further as the Post-Graduate Evening College offering M.Sc. Chemistry and M.Sc. Computer science courses. Impressive buildings have been constructed with lightning speed. His brother S.Mohamed Aslam looks after the Industrial Trading Institute. Electric power bills of all the mosques of Adirampattinam are still born by the M.K.N. Madrasa Trust.Haji A.M. Shamsuddin took over as secretary and correspondent in the year 1992. Under his administration many new buildings were built and the college received a new look. He built a separate building for the Ṣalahiya Arabic Madrasa inside the Khadir Mohideen College campus.[61]

All these educational and religious institutions could not have seen the light of the day but for the Philanthropy of M.K.N. brothers. In his welcome Address, on the occasion of the college inauguration, S.M.S. Shaik Jalaludeen, rightly asked, "But for the munificent donation of this family whoever could have dreamt of the possibility of opening a college in this place?"[62] Prof. T.Dhanakoty in 1963, the then Principal had made a remark that Adirampattinam due to constructive effort of the great M.K.N. brothers, far from being an obscure hamlet, now occupies a proud place in the educational map of Madras, say India.[63]

The Progress of the Khadir Mohideen College

To begin with, the Khadir Mohideen College was established in an asbestos shed only. During the period 1955-57, the college functioned as a Second Grade College. From June 1957 onwards it was raised to the status of a First Grade College. This college was first affiliated to the University of Madras till the establishment of the Bharathidasan University in 1982.

The College was started with 151 students in Pre-University course and in the very next year B.A., History degree course was added. Gradually in due course other B.A., B.Sc., degree courses were started. The College has now the courses of Study at the Degree level are B.A. (History), B.A. (Economics), B.B.A, B.Com, B.Sc. (Maths), B.Sc. (computer science) B.Sc. (Chemistry) and B.Sc. (Zoology). In Postgraduate level M.Sc. (chemistry), M.Sc. (zoology) M.Com are offered. In the Evening College the following courses M.Sc., (Bio-Chemistry), M.Sc., (Chemistry), M.Sc., (Computer Science), M.S., (Information Technology), M.C.A, P.G.D.C.A, B.Com., B.Sc., (Computer Science), B.Sc., (Industrial Electronics), M.phil., (Chemistry), M.phil., (Commerce), Ph.D., (Chemistry) Ph.D., (Commerce) etc., are offered. In the year 1992 the college enrolled girls and became a co-education institution. The total strength of the college in 2002-03 was 1,677 (excluding Evening College). In that there were 1,156 boys and 521 girls. Among these there were 355 Muslims boys and 37 Muslim girls.

The doors of the College are open to all without distinction of caste, creed and colour. Though the college belongs to minority Muslim community most of the students of this college belong to Hindu community. The College Mosque, Library, the college Auditorium and the playground offer greater facilities for the spiritual, intellectual and physical development of the students. Nearly 2000 pupils are studying in this college (including Evening College) but only around 400 boys and girls belong to the Muslim community.

Industrial Training Institute (I.T.I.)

The opening of I.T.I from the academic year 1984-85 satisfied a long felt need of the local people. There are three types of courses in the institution. They are Electrician and Radio and T.V. Training. The duration of the course is only two years. 36 students are on roll. The Welder Training has 36 Students in the list. There are two sections and the duration of the course is one year. In the Diesel Mechanic course 32 students are enrolled and the duration is one year. The name of the institution is Saduliya Industrial Training Institute.

REFERENCES

1. *District Census Hand Book, Tiruchirappalli, 1901-70,* Chap. VII, p. 41, Tamil Nadu Archives (T.N.A).
2. *Ibid.*
3. *Ibid.*
4. *Ibid,* p. 42.
5. *Ibid.*
6. *Ibid,* p. 43.
7. *Ibid.*

8. *Ibid*, p. 44.
9. *Ibid.*
10. *Ibid.*
11. Lewis Moore, M.C.S, *A Manual of the Trichinopoly District in the Presidency of Madras*, 1878, p.331, T.N.A.
12. *District Census Hand Book, Tiruchirappalli, 1901-70*, Chap. VII, p. 44, T.N.A.

Number of Secondary Schools

Agency	**Number of Elementary Schools**		
	1930-31	**1950-51**	**1959-60**
Government	1	6	7
Others	19	75	115
Total	**20**	**81**	**122**

Number of Students attending Secondary Schools

Agency	**Number of Elementary Schools**		
	1930-31	**1950-51**	**1959-60**
Boys	8,114	28,183	49,447
Girls	796	7240	16682
Total	**8,910**	**35,423**	**66,129**

13. *Ibid.*
14. Lewis Moore, M.C.S, *A Manual of the Trichinopoly District in the Presidency of Madras*, 1878, p. 330, T.N.A.
15. *Ibid.*, p. 333.
16. F.R.Hemingway, *Madras District Gazetteers, Trichinopoly District, 1907*, Part-II, Chap-X, Education, p. 203, T.N.A.
17. *Ibid.*
18. *Ibid.*, p. 204.
19. *Ibid.*
20. *Ibid.*, p. 205.
21. *Ibid.*
22. *Ibid.*, p. 206.
23. *Ibid.*, p. 207.

24. *Ibid.*, p. 208.
25. *District Census Hand Book, Tiruchirappalli, 1901-70*, Chap. VII, p.43, T.N.A.
26. *Ibid.*
27. *Ibid.*, p. 44.
28. *Ibid.*
29. *District Census Hand Book, Tiruchirappalli, 1901-70*, Chap. VII, p. 44, T.N.A.
30. *Viscountes Corshan Muslim Girl's School Records*, Tiruchirappalli.
31. *Syed Murthuza Government Higher Secondary School Records*, Tiruchirappalli.
32. *Ibid.*
33. *Ibid.*
34. *Khaja Mian Higher Secondary School Records*, Tiruchirappalli.
35. *Jamal Mohammed College Golden Jubilee Souvenir, 2001.*
36. *Ibid.*
37. *Ibid.*
38. *Ibid.*
39. *Ibid.*
40. *Jamal Mohammed College Magazine, 2002-03.*
41. *Ibid.*
42. *District Census Hand Book Thanjavur,1901-70*, chap- VII, p.33, T.N.A
43. *Ibid.*
44. *Ibid.*, p. 34.
45. B.S. Baliga, (Curator, Madras Record Office, Egmore), *Tanjore District Hand Book*, 1957, p.276, T.N.A.
46. F.R.Hemingway, ICS, *Madras District Gazetteers*, Tanjore, 1906, (Edited by Francis, ICS) Education, p.160, T.N.A.
47. *Ibid.*
48. *Ibid.*
49. F.R. Hemingway, ICS, *Madras District Gazetteers*, Tanjore, 1906, (Edited by Francis, ICS) Education, p.161, T.N.A.
50. *District Census Hand Book, Thanjavur, 1901-70*, Chap. VII, p. 34, T.N.A.

51. *Ibid.*
52. *Ibid.*, p. 35
53. *Ibid.*
54. *Ibid.*
55. *Ibid.*, p. 36
56. *Ibid.*
57. *M.K.N. Madrasa Trust Records.*
58. *Arivukkalanjiyam, Op. Cit.*, p. 198.
59. *Ibid.*
60. *Khadir Mohideen College Calendar*, 1982, p. 14.
61. *Ibid.*, p.15.
62. *Khadir Mohideen College Magazine,* Vol. I, 1957, p. 55.
63. *Khadir Mohideen College Magazine,* Vol. III, 1965, p. 1. *Ibid.*, p. 33.

CHAPTER

Socio-economic Changes and the Empowerment of the Muslims

Education is the cornerstone upon which the entire structure of action and thought of a nation is based. The society is claimed to be more civilized only when it has literary development. Islam recognized the extraordinary significance of education. Education has a vital role to play in the socio-economic life of the people. A discussion on the socio-economic changes took place in Tiruchirappalli and Thanjavur districts in particular and all over the Muslim community of Tamil Nadu in general and also Muslim female education and their empowerment forms the main focus of this chapter.

In a plural society such as that of India, the State generally faces demands from various castes, tribal, religious and gender groups for social Justice. Amongst such groups in India, the scheduled castes and the scheduled tribes are treated as deserving castes for concessions for historical reasons and on this a national consensus has emerged. Next to these schedule castes and schedule tribes, the most deserving group of people deserving such concessions is Muslims, because of their educational and economic backwardness. Amongst the population of India 15 to 20 per cent of people are living under poverty line in other than the Muslim community, whereas in Muslim community nearly 50 per cent of the people are living under poverty line. Moreover, in India especially in Tamil Nadu the Muslim population has converts mostly from the backward classes of people only. The reason that can be laid for the less literacy rate among the Muslims at par with the Christians can be attributed to the Missionaries whose vision and mission helped the Christians to rise amidst all odds in live.

The people who converted to Islam or to Christianity belonged to the same Indian stock. There are no such missionary activities as found in the Christian community in the Muslim community to uplift their creed. Those missionaries not only gave them education but also made the Christians to follow the culture and style of living of the Englishmen. But Muslims had a strong aversion for the English education because of the fear psychosis that this education may teach them activities against their religious faith and fervour. They were patriotic too because of their denial to imitate or follow the Englishmen, as they wanted to stick to 'Indianism' and 'Islamism'.

If there had been such activities of the missionaries among the Muslim community, then it would have been a major turn among the Muslims and the literacy rate sure would have surely increased as it has in the Christian community. Therefore the Muslims' educational and economic development should be placed at par with social Justice Groups.

Generally education has got its social and economic significance. Any society, however backward, always possessed some scientific knowledge and technical advancement. Likewise Muslims also had such back ground, but it was not so developed like that of the Westerners. "How could an education system (Madrasa educational system of the medieval period) that served the changing socio-economic and political needs of India for over six centuries (1206–1857) become so irrelevant in the contemporary times? If the education and the method of education were faulty, as observed by Moulana Abul Kalam Azad, how could their products bring about such revolutions to reach the highest officials under the king? Where were Abul Fazl and Faizi educated? And Nizam-ul-Mulk Tusi? Were not these people holding the reigns of administration so much as to leave an abiding stamp on it? Can we ignore the land survey and settlement systems started under Sher Shah Suri and completed in Akbar's reign, which still serve as basis of our land settlement? It produced scientists and planners many other talented people, not only in arts and literature, but also in the secular administration of this country."[1] From the above-mentioned statement, the Indians or the Muslims were no way inferior to any body in their intellectual activities. The further advancement in the intellectual field stagnated during the transitional period 'i.e. from mediaeval period to modern period.' What efforts to be taken to remove this state of condition? First of all the Muslims' basic misconception on the Westerners should be removed and that was achieved because of the introduction of English language. On reading the far advanced English literature, the Muslims developed a fashion and passion for reading. The British thought that the introduction of English education was the best way to introduce Western culture. But it was a wrong belief. One cannot give up his faith and his culture just because of reading English. This misbelief was also in the minds of the Muslims, which made them refuse the western education.

The social and historical factors speak about the Muslims' attitude towards Modern education based on religious ground and the Muslims of Tamil Nadu were not an exception to this. The objective of a young Hindu was to obtain education, which would fit him for a Government job or a professional career whereas a young Muslim on the other hand was not allowed to turn his mind to the secular instruction, until he had acquired sacred learning of Quran. Therefore, a Muslim boy enters school later than the Hindu boy. But this practice among the Muslims was modified by the efforts taken by the elites and the educationists of the society. This is a turning point in the educational development of the Muslims.

Educational development of the Muslims in Tamil Nadu has not only given shape to their political, socio-economic and cultural institutions, but also moulded their character and outlook on life.

The introduction of Modern Education in India effected revolutionary changes in the socio-economic and political life of Indian people. It brought rationalistic ideas and non-religious values among the Indian masses. The introduction of western medical service, population control, growth of technical education, industrial development, agricultural development and growth of trade and commerce were some of the benefits of introduction of modern education in India. It checked the backward ideas of the conservative and orthodox Hindu and Muslim people. The changes effected due to the introduction of Modern education among the Hindus are applicable to the Muslims also, except one or two exemptions. The very introduction of Modern education was a revolutionary one because it was introduced against the will of the Ulemma and the conservative Muslims. It put an end to the domination of the Ulemma in the socio economic and educational activities, opened new vistas of life and initiated modernisation in the life of the Muslims.

Regarding the socio-economic changes as a sequel to the spread of Modern education among the Muslims of Tamil Nadu especially of Tiruchirappalli and Thanjavur districts are concerned, a very useful comparative analysis of the conditions present some 50 years ago with the conditions prevailing now has been made.

Tiruchirappalli and Thanjavur districts come under the fertile Kavery Delta region. So, most of the Muslims in these districts are agriculturists. Next to agriculture, trading is the main occupation of the Muslims. Besides this the Muslims are seeking their fortunes in foreign countries mostly as petty shopkeepers and menial servants. Government jobs were not preferable among the Muslims of these regions. Apart from this majority of the Muslim people are working in farms, tanneries, beedi industries and other industries as labourers.

In coastal areas, the Muslims engage themselves in fishing profession also. Due to their poverty the Muslims even work on daily wage basis and do all sorts of works. Some 30 years back illiteracy was widespread and very common among the Muslims of this area. Even though Thanjavur always stood first in literacy among the other districts of the State, the literacy of the Muslims of this region was in a pitiable condition and Female education had no place among them. The Muslim parents considered that it was a sin to send their daughters to schools and colleges for learning. It was very rare to see a girl with eighth standard qualification and a boy with S.S.L.C qualification. Their economic condition also was very poor. Thanks to the efforts taken by the elites and the philanthropists of Tiruchirappalli and Thanjavur districts, the modern education has gradually spread among the Muslims and brought many changes in their life. The common Muslim people also understood the indispensability of the Modern Education and began to learn it. In due course they very well realized that without education, the future of their children will be miserable and the illiteracy prevailing among them will jeopardize their socio-economic and political activities. To testify the changes effected among the Muslims of Tiruchirappalli and Thanjavur districts, Adirampattinam, a majority Muslim town in this region has been taken as a case study. The researcher had conducted a survey and personal interviews with people of the town to understand the real conditions of the Muslims of this area.

First of all, the spread of Modern education has brought an appreciable change in the life style and status of the Muslims of Adirampattinam, contrary to that of prevailing three decades ago. Their dress and manners got refined. One could see distinctly the difference between an educated Muslim and an illiterate Muslim in his way of approach and behaviours. The Muslims of this locality both women and men used to wear lungies as their common dress. Now these lungies were replaced by modern dresses like Pants and Chudidars. Even the purdah system has received a modification. The Women used to wear a very big white cloth as purdah, which was most uncomfortable one. Now they are using modern 'burkhas', which is a comfortable long coat. As a result of their progress of education and improved economic condition the Adirampattinam Muslims began to derive the utility of the modern household things and equipments. The recent survey conducted by Adirai Educational Trust, a social welfare organization which is running a Matriculation school, reveals that nearly 41 per cent of the families have Telephone facility, 46 per cent of the houses have Televisions and 28 per cent of the houses have Fridge facilities and 8 per cent of the families have computers at their home. The data collected reveals that the above-mentioned facilities are found with families of good educational background.[2]

The spread of Modern education has increased the average marriage age of the Muslim boys and girls. Previously girls got married in the age of fifteen or sixteen and boys in the age of twenty. Now the educated girls and boys do marry only after their studies, at the age of twenty and twenty-six respectively. Because of their education the young generation of Adirampattinam received an enlightenment regarding male and female relationship. As a consequence the dowry evil has considerably declined. An educated girl is most preferred than an uneducated girl in the marriage market. Some twenty or twenty five years back the Muslim parents considered that it was a sin to send their daughters to schools and Colleges after attaining the age of puberty. Now this opinion has tremendously changed; most of the parents are sending their daughters to schools and colleges for learning. Now only they have understood that an educated woman could look after her family in a better way than an uneducated woman.

Once the Muslims of Adirampattinam thought that the religious education (Madarasa education) alone was enough for their children. This attitude has been changed now; they realized the indispensability of the modern education and sending their daughters to educational institutions even outside their locality. A Muslim lady named Thahira Ammal contested in the local body election and became the chairperson of the local self-government (town panchayat) and another lady named Sabeera Banu who did her civil engineering course, now engaged herself in building construction and architect and earning equal to a male engineer. Another girl named Thasleema who obtained her M.A., M. Phil., in English literature is working as Lecturer in Khadir Mohideen College of Adirampattinam. More than a dozen ladies are working as teachers in Imam Shafi Matriculation and Higher Secondary School, Adirampattinam. These are all a few examples pointed out here for the empowerment attained by the ladies of this area. These kinds of situation or incidents were unimaginable some twenty years back in this region and this shows that the Muslim women have begun to involve themselves in political and administrative fields, which is mainly due to the spread of education among them. In the survey conducted by the researcher a number of Muslim women enthusiastically expressed that their life became more meaningful after getting education. They also said that wide propagation through educational conferences and seminars to be conducted to make the Muslim women to understand the importance of education.

Even though Islam is a rational religion, some how or other irrational beliefs and practices crept in to the Muslim community in the name of religion. 'Dargha' (tomb of saints) worshiping cult is one of such unIslamic practices developed among the Muslims. This Dargha cult is against the monotheism of Islam. This practice is very common in Tiruchirappalli and Thanjavur districts. As a result of the spread of the Modern education, scientific thinking and right religious understanding have sprang-up among the educated youth and they began to question the authenticity of the Dargha cult. Because of the opposition raised by the educated mass and well-learned religious scholars, now-a-days the Dargha worship is getting unpopular among the Muslims. Tamil Nadu Thouhit Jamath, led by P.Jainul Abidin, an Aalim (religious scholar) and Tamil Nadu Muslim Munnetra Kazhagam led by Professor Zawahirullah (Islamiah College, Vaniyambadi) are the two parties with their well-educated followers vehemently working for the above-mentioned cause. They have successfully drawn the attention of the political parties and the State Government towards them and their demands. Thus a political awakening has been evolved among the Muslims especially among the young generation. This is one of the impacts of spread of Modern education.

The spread of education among the Muslim youth has broadened their social outlook and we could see more young people engage themselves in social service activities. For example, a charity endowment, namely 'Adirai Baithulmal', has been established by the educated youth of Adirampattinam working in foreign countries to help the poor people of Adirampattinam region. They collect 'Jakkath' (religious tax) and alms from the Muslims working in the foreign countries and rich people and distribute it among the poor people. They also extend interest free loans to the needy people.[3] The researcher himself was the Secretary of this Organization from 1992 to 1996.This kind of endowment is established also in more parts of Tamil Nadu.

The spread of Modern education has brought social reforms among the Muslims of Adirampattinam against the superstitious beliefs and practices prevailed among them in the name of religion. For example, previously the Maraikkayars of Adirampattinam kept themselves aloof from the rest of the Muslims of Tamil Nadu in marriage alliance and inter mingling. They strictly follow the Shafi school of thought (There are four school of thoughts found among the Muslims of the world) and do marriages among themselves only. The educated youth of this town has broken this barrier and do marriages outside and with people of other school of thoughts (the Researcher himself is an example to this; he has married a Marraikkayar girl from Adirampattinam). Moreover the Muslims of Adirampattinam followed unnecessary and unIslamic rituals (which can not be described here in detail) during their marriage ceremony and the marriages were held for three consecutive days. These practices have disappeared now because of the efforts taken by the educated youth of this place. This sort of enlightenment, inquisitive mind and questioning the unreasonable practices are developed in them because of their growth of literacy.

The most appreciable social change brought by the Modern education is the literacy of women folk. Some twenty or twenty five years back it was very rare to see a girl with eighth standard qualification. An educated young female generation with scientific and rational approach towards the day-to-day life has come up now. A social awareness about the education has developed among the Muslim women of Adirampattinam. The Muslim students who studied at Khadir Mohideen Schools and College have brought laurels to their institutions.[4] In the convocation conducted in Khadir Mohideen College, Adirampattinam in the year 2004, 101 Muslim boys 26 girls received their graduate degrees and 37 Muslim boys and 6 girls received their post graduate degrees. A Muslim student from Khadir Mohideen College got Russian Government scholarship, went to Russia and did his M.D., in medicine. To our surprise two ladies studied medicine and became Doctors, this state of affair is unimaginable some twenty five years ago.[5] Thus, a social awareness about the education has noticeably increased among the Muslims is proved without any iota of doubt.

A survey conducted by the Adirai Educational Trust (the researcher himself was one of the members of the survey team) shows that the reasons for the dropouts from schools and colleges are due to ignorance, religious reason, attaining the age of puberty, housework, early marriage and poverty. Among the above said reasons, poverty still remains and stands first and foremost cause for the discontinuation of the students from the schools and colleges. In our survey, the people of Adirampattinam expressed that a college for women with affordable expense would induce and increase more families to educate their daughters.

As far as the economic changes are concerned the spread of education has got its special impact. Even though the Muslims of these regions are economically backward but when compared with their previous condition they are in a better status now; this credit goes to the spread of education among them only. Once the Muslims of these districts were working in the foreign countries for a meager salary, which vary from Rs.5000 to 8000. Now, their educational and professional qualifications gave them a raised economic status. Previously most of them went to Gulf and South East Asian countries as contract labourers. But now they are going to Western countries like USA, Canada, England and Australia to seek their fortunes because of their professional and technical qualifications.

The young educated people who are well settled in foreign countries have developed among them a farsightedness, philanthropic attitude and a social responsibility. To give an example to this, the alumni of Jamal Mohammed College who are working in foreign countries had donated large sum to their Alma mater. We could see some of the buildings in Jamal Mohammed College are built with their assistance. The Muslim students who obtained technical qualifications have become industrial owners and they are using modern technical development in their industries and are able to give employment opportunities to hundreds of young people.[6] The industries especially the tanneries owned by the Muslims once had old methods of production. But after gaining modern technical know-how, their industries got modernized and the production increased so that their economic status has improved a lot.

Some 20 or 25 years ago only a very few Muslims were working in the government departments. Previously the Muslims had a dislike for the Government service. The education has changed their attitude and now the Muslims have developed a liking for Government jobs and they are competing in equal terms with others in public service examinations and occupying key administrative posts and high ranks in the police department too. The credit goes to the efforts of the philanthropists, Government attitude and in consequence of the spread of education.

A self financed college called Dawood Batcha College for Arts and Science has been founded at Rajagiri, a village near Thanjavur by a gentleman named Dawood Batcha. After obtaining his degree from Jamal Mohammed College Tiruchirappalli, he went to Singapore to seek his fortune and earned a lot of money there. He spent all his earnings for the establishment of this college. In Tirchy city a women college named AIMAN College for Women had been established in the year 2000 by the Abuthabi Indian Muslim Association is an another mile stone in the educational development of the Muslims, especially in the women's education. Yet another college named Nainar Mohammed College for Arts and Science has been established recently at Aranthangi, a taluk headquarters. Like this there are Engineering colleges and polytechnics established by the Muslims all over Tamil Nadu. These developments and philanthropic munificence shows that the Muslims have come up from their old beliefs and began to make use of their wealth for the cause of education.

In the political field also the Muslims make their claims for due place. Political awareness has aroused among the Muslims in the recent years due to the spread of education. The Tamil Nadu Muslim Munnetra Kazhagam (T.M.M.K.) led by a learned Professor Zawahirullah of Islamiah college of Vaniyambadi and Tamil Nadu Thouhit Jamath (T.N.T.J.) led by an Aalim (Religious Scholar) P.Jainul Abidin are the two movements working for the cause of the Muslim's empowerment in the political field in the recent years. Educated Muslim youth rallied under their leadership demanding reservation for the Muslim community in Government jobs, Legislative assembly and Parliament.

For a long time the Muslims had a wrong notion on the Family-planning scheme of the government. The educational progress has made them understand the advantages of small family norms and now-a-days they are co-operating and at the same time not deviating from the Islamic principles with the government. For example, previously in Adirampattinam, every family had four or five children but now-a-days they have one or two children only. In the year 2004, the total number of birth was 311 among this Muslims were 178, the total number of death was 115 among this Muslims were 76. For the last two decades as derived from the rough estimate of the records of the Town Panchayat and Directorate of Census Operations, the birth rate of Adirampattinam has decreased but at the same time the death rate has also decreased because of the advancement of medical facilities, due to this the population has increased.[7] As a result of the observation of small family scheme their economic status and the educational condition have received an appreciable improvement.

The advantages of the knowledge of the English to the Muslims were almost immeasurable. Only after learning English, the Muslims came to know the wrong interpretations and distortion of the History of India. The Muslims tried to remove the biased views of the British and successfully rectified it. The Modern education has brought a revival in the thought process of the Muslims (i.e.) from mediaevalism to modernism. The Nationalist spirit of the Muslims went to a high proportion only after learning Modern education. The Muslims understood that their fear psychosis was quiet wrong, which was a result of their ignorance. To acquire knowledge the caste, creed, race and language should not be a barrier.

The Muslim's knowledge on modern democracy, science and arts was enriched because of the Modern education. The Indian literature of both Hindus and Muslims did not include any idea on nationalism but was known to them only after the introduction of the modern education. It was inevitable and can be historically explained by the fact that due to economic backwardness, the Muslims were not socially or politically integrated into a nation. The Muslims not only reinforced their knowledge enormously but also developed a broad outlook and perspective of the world. The Muslims involved themselves in the National freedom struggle in a better way because of the awareness they got from the learning of higher education. Even though the Muslims felt difficulties in the beginning to have English as the medium of instruction, but in due course they adapted themselves and got empowered in the English language.

Female Education and Empowerment

The planned economic development envisaged an all around socio-economic progress without showing disparity to anybody. However, gender inequality and gender bias continue to exist in society especially in Muslim community. But Islam protects the rights of womanhood by giving economic liberty and other privileges to them. Inequality syndrome further manifests itself in the form of social indicators like sex ratios, low literacy, female infanticide, morbidity and mortality amongst a girl child, all these things brings down the status and the empowerment of women.

The propriety of making literacy was the soul test of education. It would be a monstrous error to consider the Muslim womanhood as uneducated because they were not given the opportunity for a long time to get educated themselves, so it is right to call them as non educated. When a man got education, the illiteracy in him is eradicated where as when a woman got education the illiteracy in her and of her family is eradicated. A woman's part in her husbands avocation is at best small; and the higher her social rank, and easier her worldly circumstances, the smaller it becomes. The question of women's education was the most serious and pressing problem that has to be tackled by the Muslim community with zeal and earnestness.

Islam gives equal emphasis and importance on the education of both the male and female. One half of the community consists of women and that they have every right against men, even as men have rights against the women. This phenomenon is not fully realized by the Muslim community, even at this late hour. One could not help a suspicion that in many a case a daughter appears in school and returns merely as an advertisement of the liberalism of her parent. Even today, there are some conservative Muslims and Ulemma who refused to give higher education to their Muslim girls. More than 95 per cent of the Muslim women remain without education, what hope is there to them to solve the social and economic problems of the Muslim community? This state of condition is commonly prevailing among the Muslims of Tiruchirappalli and Thanjavur districts, which will be changed only by the efforts and self-realization of the Muslims of these regions.

The right of women and their empowerment within the Islamic framework is a recent topic. However, it will help one to have a clear idea when pertinently examine the packages of rights that Islam grants to the Muslim women. Although Islam grants women a comprehensive package of rights, ignorance of Islamic tenets and lack of education and insistence of the society on using outdated non-Islamic and discriminatory cultural practices has led to the oppression of Muslim women. This state of condition remains with Muslim women mainly due to the non-education. The Muslim Shariah declares that the women have the right to life and education, right to worship and spiritual development, right to self-respect and kind treatment, right to choose her husband, right to have economic independence, right to make stipulation in her marriage contract, right to retain her identity, right to consortium, consultation and expression, right to have property, protection against slander and physical abuse, right to shelter as a divorcee and widow's maintenance right and remarriage.

It is a sad state that the Muslim women are not given the proper guidance and knowledge about the rights in Islam. All these rights are in theories, because the man being the breadwinner decides the way the woman has to lead her life. She is not aware of the rights that Islam has endowed her with. She is kept in darkness and ignorance. But according to Islam, rights and responsibilities of both sexes are equitable and balanced in their totality. Islam wishes to produce a woman who is not only independent in personality, but also one who does not feel deficient, because she is a female. Islam seeks to develop the personality, which gives women the confidence, security and esteem to deal with men as equals without having to play to their gallery or aspire to behave like them. Empowerment as the word denotes is linked to knowledge and making decisions that shape one's life.

One can trace the historical precedents for Muslim women's empowerment in the historical past. The Medina society being the first Islamic community set the tone for Muslim women's empowerment because women played important roles in the development of Islam. Muslim women in Medina played important leadership roles and worked alongside their men to promote the Islamic state. They attended the mosques to pray and listened to the sermons, took lessons from the Prophet (Pbuh) and sought his advice in public and personal issues. Hafsa (Rali), the daughter of Caliph Umar was entrusted with the responsibility of collecting various items on which the Quran was compiled. Women in Medina performed the Hajj alongside the men, recited the Quran and were versatile in the Knowledge of Shariah. Aiysha (Rali), the Prophet's wife was an expert in Hadith (traditions of the Prophet). To contradict the history, Muslim men of today's world argue that it is un-Islamic for women to work outside the house, some even deny women their right to education by prohibiting them from attending schools and colleges to acquire knowledge and Islam is cited as the basis of such restrictions. They do not appreciate the fact that education is essential for all Muslims be they, men, women, disabled and all.

There is a vital difference between a Muslim woman and a Hindu woman. A Muslim should follow 'Purdah system' as ordained by God. There will be no relaxation on it. But this should not stand as a hurdle in the empowerment of the Muslim women. Purdah will not stand as a curtain in acquiring education. Going to schools or colleges with purdah will not hinder their studies. Even today we could see so many Muslim girls practicing purdah and attending schools and colleges without any hesitation. Today one could see Christian Nuns practicing purdah and doing their work. Purdah is taken wrongly as closing even the face of a girl, which is not correct. But some Muslim girls are practicing it without any proper knowledge of its purpose and its usage. Muslim girls are free to take up education because Islam stresses importance equally on both men and women in acquiring education.

Some twenty years back the Muslims of Adirampattinam rarely appreciates an educated Muslim woman and in turn she becomes only the cynosure of the society and not the asset of the community. But when compared to the previous generation the present educated young generation has become very much aware of the fact that Islam is not denying education to them; only some people in the society is enforcing it on them. The spread of education has emboldened them to raise questions against the abuses on them. Though the Muslim girls of Adirampattinam have far advanced than their conditions some twenty or twenty-five years back, they have yet several miles to go! Even now their educational status and empowerment is below average only. There remain still a lot of girls without attaining the benefit of the education. The elites of Adirampattinam should take efforts to bring them under the main stream of education. The process has already started on this matter; there is a move among the elites and the philanthropists of Adirampattinam to establish a college for women.

To appreciate the upcoming awareness and sudden spurt in the search of education in the Muslim womanhood, all the pioneers who sowed the seed of interest and etiquette, should be gratefully remembered for their wonderful job. To our surprise the first Muslim school established in 1917 in Tiruchirapplli city was (Viscountes Corshan girls school) for the girls only. The one thing that should be considered as the need of the hour is that the religious heads or the Imams, Moulvis and the elites of the society need to come forward to make the community aware of their rights and duties. The various Islamic groups should organize seminars, workshops, paper presentation, awareness programmes, young men associations and women clubs to educate the people, so that they know their responsibilities and rights to make them capable of analyzing issues with the help of Shariah before making judgements.

Regarding the literacy of the Muslim women there was a wrong opinion prevailing. Literacy and education are two different things. We could see in Adirampattinam and Tiruchirappalli regions Muslim women reciting Quran, reading Urdu and Arab-Tamil (Tamil version in Arabic script). This could also be taken as a development of literacy. In the opinion of the researcher, literacy means not just knowing, English, Tamil or Western Science alone; it means to read and write in any language or to have knowledge about things through some language. If it is so then there are more people to be considered literate among Muslims, because there is lot of people who could read 'Quran' (but could not write). Among Urdu speaking people there are so many women who could read and write Urdu. If we take this point in to consideration, then there will be more literate men and women in the Muslim community of Tamil Nadu.

As according to the census of 1891 in literacy rate, the Christians came first and then the Mohammedans. Among the Hindus, who formed of course the majority of the population, 85 per cent out of every 100 males were unable to read and write. As regard to female education the Christians were far ahead of the other creeds. The Musalman females showed the next best results, though a long interval separated them from their Christian sisters. But they were better than their Hindu sisters. It is a common belief that Muslims are not as well educated as Hindus but this is erroneous, when compared to these three religious groups, Christians, Muslims and Hindus on the basis of population ratio. These statistics however refer only to elementary education. When coming to the point of higher education things are different. The

Muslim women opting for higher education are very low in those days as well as today. But due to the encouragement and efforts taken by Muslim educationalists the conditions are improving slowly.

The female education was for many years, as observed from the sketch history of education, almost entirely in the hands of the various Missionary societies. Of late, secular schools had sprung up in the various parts of the Madras Presidency. The Maharaja's schools which were established under the patronage of the rulers of Northern Circars were later changed over under the management of Madras branch of National Indian Association and they received aid from the state, and the rest though unaided were under inspection, and asked to furnish returns about 15 years ago, a Government normal school during its existence educated only 60 Hindus and no Muslim boys or girls and the native Christians were teachers. So, it was reorganized to fulfill the object for which it was originally started. The Government undertook the charge of few elementary schools for girls, which were established by some Local Fund Boards and Municipalities. After this measure, there was a considerable increase of strength of the girls of all religions, especially of Muhammadan girls. The Government took care, not to interfere with the efforts taken by the private bodies. Because of this policy, there were 35 such schools established at the close of 1884-85, 3 in South Arcot, 4 in North Arcot, 4 in Tanjore and others else were in Madras Presidency.[8]

The British Government evinced an equally keen interest in the education of Muslim girls. In January 1875, a committee presided over by Lady Hobart discussed the question of the education of Muslim girls. It proposed to encourage the womenfolk by promoting the establishment of schools in which the girls were to be taught in their own language, needle work of every description and other industrial occupations.[9] On 16th April, 1875 a school was opened at Royapettah, Madras by the prince of Arcot with 24 pupils.[10] The news of the inauguration of the school hit the headline in Muslim newspaper. They eulogized the services of Lady Hobart for the cause of Muslim women's education. It pointed out that, because of her initiative there was 'friendly intercourse between the native and European ladies'.[11] The sensible ones among the Muslims sent in application for the admission for their daughters and the number of applications was disproportionate to the seats available.[12]

Lord Hobart who took a keen and warm interest in Muslim education, died a few days later and the committee, as attribute to his memory and recognition of the role of Lady Hobart in the establishment of the school, called it 'Hobart school'. Lady Hobart gave the school a donation of Rs 10,000 and on 7th December 1875 the Princess of Tanjore visited the institution and donated RS 7000 towards its support. Although most of the children belonged to the poorer class, their parents would not allow them to walk through the streets woven in Purdah and it was found necessary to hire five carts with female attendants to convey the students to and from the school.13 When a cart driver employed to convey the students, seduced a girl student then the school suffered loss of prestige and there was a sudden fall in the admission.14 To start with the school functioned only as an elementary school. In 1880 it was raised to a high school.15 In 1885 a training class was added with the help of additional aid from the Government.16 But, subsequently the committee managing the school found in difficult to meet its increasing expenditure with its limited income and proposed that the Government should take it over.17

The role of the National Indian Association in the cause of Muslim women's education was significant. The Madras branch of this Association was established in 1875. The patron was the Governor, the vice president was T.Muthu Sammy Iyer, the secretary was Mrs. Brander, the treasurer was Mir Humayun Shah Bahadur.[18] The chief means employed by this branch to encourage Muslim women's education were grants to scholarships to Muslim girls, prizes to school girls and some special scholarships given to girls of Hobart schools.

An English woman, named Fowbr was engaged to give home tuition to Muslim girls.[19] But despite the endeavour of a few enlightened persons to promote the cause of Muslim women's education there was no interest from with in to educate their children, particularly girls. The number of dropouts even from the few schools that existed was alarming. For instance two girls' schools at Mayuram and Tanjore had to be closed for want of pupils. "The population mostly consists of Labbais who are most indifferent to education", observed the frustrated Director of Public Instruction in his letter to the Government.[20] But this was not the case everywhere. An educated Muslim Government official started a girls' school at Wallajahpet on his own in 1889 with five girls. With in two years the strength grew to forty. When the strength grew unexpectedly the founder requested the Government to take over the school, as he was unable to manage it on his own. The Government also willingly took it over.[21]

The Christian missionaries were also active in the field of education. Many Hindu and Muslim girls' schools were established by them. They were referred to as Zenana schools. Naturally the syllabi and instruction were Christian oriented. There was much opposition in Muslim quarters in sending their girls to the Christian schools.[22] The editor of Alhami, a popular Muslim newspaper advised the Muslims to start their own schools and said "it is such to regretted that native nobles and gentleman unhesitatingly spend thousands of rupees on debaucher but are reluctant to help in the establishment of useful institutions such as school."[23] Another editor of a Muslim paper, giving expression to the typical attitude of Muslims, asserted that female education was unnecessary and educated females would not remain under Purdah.[24]

Three female candidates appeared for the lower secondary examination and one passed. In the previous year one candidate appeared for the examination without success. At the primary examination 37 passed for certificates out of 46 entrants, against 19 out of 46 in 1899-1900 and 37 out of 78 in 1898-99. The results of the year were thus very satisfactory, not less than 80 per cent of the entrants having qualified for certificates. Not taking into account the special schools, but including indigenous schools, the number of schools for girls was 120 with 4,547 pupils against 154 schools with 5,612 pupils in 1899-1900 and 163 schools with 5,550 pupils in the year before. The total number of girls in all classes and grades of schools fell from 17,854 to 17,329. Sixteen girls reached the lower secondary stage against nine in the previous year. In 1898-99, the girls' strength in lower secondary stage was 28.[25]

The proportion of Mohammedan girls in schools is nearly one-fourth, which is distinctly higher than that of other girls in schools in general, and there has been little variation in this proportion throughout the Quinquennium. The number of girls in school has risen therefore equally with that of boys. There has been a total gain of 3,005. There were, however, 3,524 girls in Quran schools in 1912 as against 2,317 in 1907. Girls were still almost entirely in the elementary stage of instruction, there being in 1912 only four in the secondary stage and one in the collegiate. There are now 42 Government Mohammedans Girls' schools including two training schools for mistresses.[26]

Excluding schools for special education and including indigenous schools the number of schools for girls rose from 120 with 4,547 pupils in 1900-01 to 162 with 5,472 pupils. No female candidate appeared for the matriculation examination, but all the four pupils who appeared for the lower secondary examination were successful; in the previous year one candidate passed out of 3. At the primary level examination 27 passed out of 35 appeared, while 37 passed out of 46 in 1900-01.[27]

The tendency of Muslims borne out to female education can be gauged by an instance of event that occurred in a liberal institution such as Mohammedan Anglo Oriental College where Sheik Abdullah (Baba Mian) when put forth a proposal to establish a school for the girls. He was vehemently opposed. The English Principal of MAO College adjudged that the establishment of school for girls will be detrimental to the interest of the Aligarh College and counseled that the Women's College is like the infectious and contagious diseases hospital be setup outside the premises of the Aligarh College. By the organized efforts of Shaik Abdullah a girls' school was established in 1907, which is today a unique residential institution for the female education in the sub continent.[28] More than four thousand girls from the primary to the higher level are receiving education.

The state of condition of the Mohammedan girls, as an example is taken from the Director of Public Instructions records of 1907, among 22,000 Mohammedan girls returned as receiving education 10,000 were reading in Quran schools, and 12,000 in public institutions. The later were almost entirely in the primary stage of instruction; of them nearly 5,000 were attending public schools for Mohammedan girls, and the remainder in other public schools.[29]

There had been an increase of nearly 17 per cent in the number of Mohammedan girls attending public and private institutions. The increase in the case of public institutions occurred mainly in the last year of quinquennium (1906). The Government maintains 35 schools for Mohammedan girls with strength of about 1,600.The Mohammedan girls who proceed beyond the fourth standard are numbered in tens: it stood at 29 at the beginning of the period and 57 at the end.[30] Begum Sultan Jahan, the former ruler of Bhopal, was one of the exponents who took efforts in popularizing female education among the Muslims. She also has the honour of being the first Chancellor of the Aligarh Muslim University in 1920.[31] A certain number of Muslim Women's institutions and the Anjuman-i-Islam in particular even prepared the plan for setting up a Muslim Women's University in Maharashtra and Chennai.

A separate college for Muslim Women and a Hostel attached was a longstanding demand of the Muslim community, which was reiterated by them in 1941 especially from Madras. The need for the establishment of a separate college for Muslim women had already been conceded as a post war measure and the post war period had already started by the Government. The Muslims requested to expedite the establishment of a women's college as early as possible. The Muslim community was very anxious that the college should be functioned from the next academic year (i.e.1946). The Muslims suggested that the college might be named after the name of the Governor's wife. Further the Muslims requested for the immediate inauguration of the college, the office of the Inspector General of Police might be provided as a temporary accommodation. But this request was not fulfilled, instead the Government made facilities to accommodate Muslim women students in Mohammedan college of Madras.[32]

The action of the Government in making available the existing facilities for collegiate education in the Mohammedan College to Muslim women students was a step towards the advancement of women's education, and the Muslim women students were deriving considerable advantage there from. There was no substance in the protests raised against this action; for the simple reason that no one was compelled by Government to resort to a mixed college. But this does not obviate the necessity for a separate college for Muslim women. Government was aware that, while the educated section of the Muslim community was not averse to Muslim women students taking advantage of such of the facilities as are now available in men's colleges for university education, still there was a large body of opinion in the Muslims against the principle of co-education, not only in the high school stages but also in the degree classes. It was inevitable that so far as professional courses were concerned, in the absence of separate facilities, women students must seek admission to men's Colleges, but that was not be a justification to refuse to afford, wherever possible, separate facilities, which were considered essential for women students from all points of view. It will be conceded that for the healthy development of the mental and moral faculties of women students, a free atmosphere and a freedom of movement are most desirable and such a free atmosphere and freedom can be available only in a College exclusively intended for women. The establishment of the Queen Mary's College and the women's Xian College amply testify to this fact.[33]

The establishment of Southern India Educational Trust College for Women was a further major step towards the promotion of Women's Education. In the beginning there were only 12 students joined in the college and its strength increased to 300 within few years.[34] The establishment of the college itself furnished the needed impetus to the Muslim community to send larger numbers to the college. Therefore the lack of any big strength of Muslim women students to start with, cannot furnish any valid reason for the establishment of a separate college for Muslim women. The low strength of the Muslim women students in all the colleges, together with the large number of Muslim girls who do not take to higher and collegiate education on account of the absence of a separate college for women with an Islamic atmosphere and facilities for the development of Islamic culture, would be more than to justify the need for the establishment of a separate College for Muslim women. Another so called reason said was the lack of sufficient Muslim women staff to run the separate College for Muslim women could not also stand in the way because the Muslim community expressed that it had no objection to the employment of non-Muslim women staff for the College. The purpose mentioned above was fulfilled by the establishment of South Indian Educational Trust College for women which was renamed afterwards as Basheer Ahamed Sayeed College for women.

Tamil Nadu has a minuscule Muslim minority, i.e. merely 5.75 per cent of the population. Even the Christians have with 6.5 per cent population out number the Muslims. Yet the community has invested considerable in education in order to stay on par with others in the race for development. The Organization of Muslim Educational Institutions and Association in Tamil Nadu (OMEIAT) have been striving to give a central focus to the educational struggle of the Muslims in the state.[35] The OMEIAT Directory of Muslim Educational Institutions in Tamil Nadu is the first solid outcome in this direction. In the demise of the various measures taken in the Madras Presidency during the British rule and the formation of secular India after independence the education of the Muslims stagnated without further development. The Muslim philanthropic efforts rose to the occasion and served the need of the community.

The Muslim community of Tamil Nadu has a unique characteristic feature of maintaining a humble façade with solid infrastructure in the field of education. Though the underbelly of the community still drips with poverty and educational backwardness, some philanthropists, and of late, the ones who use education for commerce, erected enough number of monuments of their munificence and enterprise respectively. No wonder than 35 lakhs strong community runs as many as 22 colleges (self-financed Arts and Science colleges are not included), a dozen Engineering Colleges and Industrial Technical Institutes, half that many Poly-techniques, 125 High Schools 152 Primary Schools and several other institutions.[36] These statistics may be impressive, but show that the pattern is top-heavy i.e., the number of schools almost competing with those of colleges and professional educational institutions. This somewhat skewed pattern does not exactly help the community to attain a balanced profile of literacy, education, skills and professionalism. There could be more useful conclusions from the data available at present.

The OMEIAT Directory fulfils the long-standing need of such a guide for the seekers of opportunities in the field of education. The Directory is though poorly edited, useful in several ways as the data is assiduously collected over several months and reflects the painstaking efforts of the minority. The flashes from an official survey provided at the end are astonishing in that it puts only two percent of the states Muslims in the upper income bracket. There are some private philanthropic associations helping the poor Muslim students by giving scholarships and loans. 'Abudhabi Indian Muslim Association (AIMAN) and Indian Muslim Association (IMAN) are the two appreciable associations functioning in Tamil Nadu. AIMAN is extending free scholarships amounting Rs.30,00,000 per annum to the poor Muslim girls and boys of various parts of Tamil Nadu. The poor Muslim students of Khadir Mohideen College, Adirampattinam had received Rupees 44,000 as scholarship from IMAN during the academic year 2000-01.[37] The AIMAN has founded a self-financed women's college in the city of Tiruchirapalli, which caters the needs of higher education of hundreds of Muslim girls.

REFERENCES

1. *'Madrasa Education in India, Its Past and Present'*, Published by Center for Research and Industrial Development, Chandigarh, 1990, Tamil Nadu Archives (T.N.A).
2. *Adirai Educational Trust Survey Report*, Adirampattinam, 2004.
3. Adirai Baithulmal, An Islamic Social Welfare Organisation, Established in 1992.
4. Mohammed Iqbal, M.Sc., Zoology, University Second Rank, 1992.

   Vahitha Banu, M.Sc., Chemistry, University Second Rank, 1998.

   Parisath Banu, M.Sc., Zoology, University Second Rank, 2000.

   Juwairia Begam, M.Sc., Zoology, University Third Rank, 2001.

   Syed Ibrahim, M.Sc., Chemistry, University Second Rank, 2001.

   S.A.Fowzia, M.Sc., Chemistry, University First Rank, 2002.

   Faizal, M.Sc., Chemistry, University Third Rank 2004.
5. Mohammed Hanus, M.D., Beach Street, Adirampattinam.

   Khamarunisa, M.B.B.S., D.G.O, Shifa Hospital, Adirampattinam.

   Abdul Latheefa, M.B.B.S., D.G.O, Private Practice, Adirampattinam.
6. Mohammed Farook, Pioneer International (Leather Products), Industrial Estate, Ranipet.
7. *Census of India 2001*, Directorate of Census Operations, Tamil Nadu, and *Town Panchayat Office Adirampattinam, 'Birth - Death' Register*, 2004.

8. *Manual of the Administration of the Madras Presidency,* 1886, Vol. II, p. 594, T.N.A.
9. *Report on Public Instruction in Madras Presidency,* 1875-76, p. 702, T.N.A.
10. *Ibid.*
11. *Shamsul-Akhbar,* 22nd March, 1875, T.N.A.
12. *Shamsul-Akhbar,* 3rd May, 1875, T.N.A.
13. *Ibid.*
14. *Safir-i-Madras,* 27th March, 1876, T.N.A.
15. *No. 71-71, Educational,* 6th February, 1896, T.N.A.
16. *No. 715, Educational,* 27th September, 1893, T.N.A.
17. *No. 318, Educational,* 26th April, 1895, T.N.A.
18. *Appendix to Education Commission Report,* 1884, p.129, T.N.A.
19. *No. 50, Educational, (misc)* 31st January, 1883, T.N.A.
20. *No. 230, Educational,* 15th January, 1896, T.N.A.
21. *No.607, Educational,* 3rd August, 1891, *Letter from D.Duncan, Acting DPI, Madras to the Chief Secretary through the Accountant General,* 18th July, 1891, T.N.A.
22. *Shamsul-Akhbar,* 15th December, 1887, T.N.A.
23. *Ai-Hami,* 22nd June, 1895, T.N.A.
24. *Tilsin-i-Haivath,* 25th March, 1889, T.N.A.
25. *Report on Public Instruction in Madras Presidency,* 1899-00, p. 35, T.N.A.
26. *Report on Public Instruction in Madras Presidency,* 1911-12, p. 56, T.N.A.
27. *Report on the Administration of Madras Presidency,* 1900-01, p. 258, T.N.A.
28. Abdullah College for Women, (Aligarh Muslim University), *College Magazine,* 1901-02.
29. *Report on Public Instruction in Madras Presidency,* 1906-07, p.52, T.N.A.
30. *Report on Public Instruction in Madras Presidency,* 1906-07, p.53, T.N.A.
31. *Aligarh Muslim University Magazine,* 1901-02.
32. *G.O. No.1480,* dated 19th September, 1945, (Memorandum presented to the Advisor to his Excellency the Governor of

Madras by the Mohammadan Educational Association of Southern India, Madras), T.N.A.

33. *Ibid.*
34. Justice Basheer Ahmed Sayeed College for Women, *Diary, 2003-04.*
35. Rahat Abrar, *OMEIAT Directory of Muslim Educational institutions in Tamil Nadu, 2000,* Muslim Education, Aligarh Publications.
36. *Ibid.*
37. AIMAN, *Indian Overseas Bank NRE Cheque No.664728,* dated 15th January 2001.

7

CHAPTER

Conclusion

Education is a composite structure of knowledge of arts, science, customs, traditions and values transmitted from preceding generation to succeeding generation. During the mediaeval period the Madarasa system of education of the Muslims remained not merely the seat of learning of the Muslims only but also that of Hindus. But, when conditions changed during the modern period, unfortunately the transmission of the Madrasa system of education to the succeeding generation was not possible due to lack of advancement in the field of education. However, education as an indicator of social well-being has increased among the Muslims after a long debate, trial and efforts of the Muslim leaders and elites of the community in the twentieth century onwards.

In India the sons of Islam were remotely removed from the rest of the Muslim world, as they could not keep pace with their brothers outside in material as well as in intellectual advancement. Consequently, their attainments in education were not as high as it was expected. During the mediaeval period India was no way lagging behind the West. This condition was reversed only in the modern period, because the East had failed to cope up with the Western advancement in science and arts.

Before the introduction of Western education almost all requirements in public and private life of the Muslims ranging from religious rituals to the functioning of the state missionary were based on the Madrasa system of education. Even among the Hindus there were many scholars and poets in Persian and Urdu language who derived their knowledge from this system of education, except the portions of learning Quran and Hadith, which were compulsory only to the Muslims. From such educational centres all kinds of knowledge were imparted to the students and hundreds of scholars and intellectuals were produced by this system. But the trend slowly changed after the dawn of modern period, there was a need for all around development in the field of education. This transition from mediaeval to modern period took place only after the advent of the Europeans in India.

The social condition and the demographic divisions of the Muslims of Tamil Nadu are different from their counterparts in North India. Among the three divisions namely the Rawthers, Maraikkayars and Deccani Urdu speaking Muslims, the first two groups are wide spread in Tamil Nadu and contributed much for the promotion of the education of the Muslims especially in Tiruchirappalli and Thanjavur districts. The Muslims of these two districts are mostly agriculturists and traders. Their wealth and philanthropic mind made them contribute liberally to the promotion of the education in these regions.

The Muslims' attitude towards Western education was very hostile in the beginning because of the social, cultural and religious reasons. The Muslims put themselves in isolation and kept away from the Western education because they felt that the British had ruined them politically by replacing them from ruling India, which made them see the British with inimical eyes. The British East India Company as a private body never took keen interest in the education of the Indians later they felt the need and took efforts to qualify the Indians for the posts of clerks. But the Muslims did not respond to it. As a consequence it affected the academic life of the Muslims. They thought that the aversion towards English men and avoidance of English language was no mean a loss to Muslims. On the contrary, the new generation of Muslims who came out of the portals and institutions of the secular education with their mindset remained altogether different from those of religious institutions? Moreover, the Muslims also thought that in the Western teaching there was no familial morals and values, fear of God thus, making the individual rigid and indifferent to the values and responsibilities towards the community. This opinion is not correct because the ethics of education are only to enlarge the horizon of knowledge and wisdom of an individual. It should not be viewed through socio-religious and cultural ethos. The Pre-British Indian educational systems of both Hindus and Muslims were primarily religious because of this reason they conceived a wrong idea on the Western education. Besides these reasons the Muslims were patriotic too.

When the British Government of India in general and the Government of Madras Presidency in particular paid more attention towards the education of the Indians, the Hindus were first to respond to it with the right spirit whereas the Muslims did not take it seriously. Because of this, they were lagging behind the Hindus in the Government appointments and other fields too. The Christian missionaries in India paid more attention to the Hindus than to the Muslims. The reason for this was the question of conversion was hardly possible with the Muslims. In spite of the lethargic response of Muslims, the Government took various measures to improve the education of the Muslims. It granted funds to start educational institutions; instituted schools specially meant for the Muslims, extended half fee concessions to the Muslim students and granted liberal scholarships from primary to the college level. Even after these measures the Muslims showed very less response. However, there was an appreciable change and advancement towards the end of the nineteenth century.

In the beginning of the twentieth century the Indian education development suffered because of the reactionary regime of Lord Curzon, but the situation changed soon after his reign. The introductions of Dyarchy in 1919, subsequently the formation of the Government in the Madras Presidency by the Justice Party were instrumental in the development of the education. The demand of the Justice party Government to transfer education as a State subject and the immediate sanction of this request by the British Government of India was an epoch-making development in the field of education. Following this, the Government encouraged the public to establish educational institutions for the people of their community. This was another turning point in the educational history of the Muslims. Many schools and colleges were started in the Madras Presidency by the Muslim philanthropists. The Government also took keen interest in the education of the Muslims, the Director of Public Instruction, the various District Collectorates and the Department of Education and Public Health were ordered to work for the development of education among the Indians in general and Muslims in particular. Due to these measures a number of schools and colleges were established all over the Madras Presidency.

There was a significant change in the attitude of the Muslims towards the Modern education. The enlightened Muslim leaders and the elites of the Muslim community propagated the importance of the Western education among the Muslims and made them to understand without its help the progress of the community is impossible. The Muslim Newspapers and Magazines did yeomen service in the promotion of education of the Muslims. They highlighted the issues and demands of the Muslims in their Newspapers and attracted the attention of the Government towards the grievances. The Muslim philanthropists founded trusts and associations for the cause of education. The entry of the philanthropic effort was a major turning point in the growth of education of the Muslims. As a consequence to their efforts there was a good response from the community. Financial help, endowment scholarships were instituted and made available to the Muslim pupils at all levels of education. The Government had sanctioned lands and sites for building schools and colleges, building grants were sanctioned to construct infrastructures for the educational institutions. Local Governments and local funds were diverted towards the development of education of the Muslims, where the Muslim population was more.

The Government orders were passed when and wherever required to implement educational reforms. The Government also paid attention to the emoluments of the teaching and non-teaching staff of the educational institutions and granted salary grants. The schools must have good teachers to teach the students otherwise the basic cause of the education will get collapsed. So, the Government allotted seats for the Muslim students in the Teacher Training schools. The Muslim inspectors both ladies and gents were appointed to supervise the Muslim educational institutions. As the Muslims attach more importance to their religion, religious instructions were allowed in the schools specially intended for the Muslims and moral instructors were appointed by the Government. Arabic and Urdu languages were taught and Urdu was allowed as the medium of instruction where the Urdu speaking people were thickly populated.

Whenever there was a problem or crisis in the field of education or some concessions taken back by the Government, the Muslim leaders appealed to the Government even fought with the Government and solved the problems or preserved the concessions which were given already. The Muslim inhabitants of a village or locality submitted their grievance petitions and memorandums to the British Government and got the things done in their favour. The old Nawabs and Princes whose dynasties were once ruling over the various fragments of the Madras Presidency also contributed their mite for the cause of education. For example, the Arcot Nawab (Azam Jha) and the Maratta Prince of Thanjavur had donated lands and extended financial support to establish Madrasas and schools for both boys and girls in their respective regions.

The efforts of British Government to improve the education of the Muslims and the response of the Muslims received a momentum in the first half of the twentieth century. An overall assessment was made with the help of all kinds of the Government records, which shows a big change in the condition of the education of the Muslims, which was far better than their condition before the implementation of the Government measures. The comparative study and analysis made on the three religious groups namely Hindus, Muslims and Christians shows that the education among the Muslim males was better than their Hindu counterparts whereas the improvement of the education of the Muslim female was not up to the expectation. For this pitiable condition of the female education, the Government could not be blamed.

The steps and measures taken by the Government in the field of education were disturbed due to the Second World War, because the Government diverted its attention and funds for the purpose of war. The freedom movement of our nation received a greater momentum during this period, so education reforms were not paid much importance. After the independence, as far as the education of the Muslims was concerned, no separate measures were taken. The free Indian Government followed the policy of secularism and the educational developments and reforms were implemented generally. At this juncture, in the absence of separate measures for the Muslims, the Muslim philanthropic magnanimity came to the rescue of the education of the Muslims.

The earliest private effort taken in 1919 in Tamil Nadu, even to say in South India was by the Vaniyambadi Muslim Educational Society. Private efforts had been revived in the middle of the twentieth century to establish educational institutions in various places of the Madras Presidency. Between 1950 and 1960 a good number of institutions in the school and collegiate levels had been established in the various districts of the Madras state to serve the need of the society.

The Muslims and Christians were given minority status in the new Constitution of India. The Christians took full advantage of the minority rights more than the Muslims. In the absence of liberal external contributions to Muslim Organisations in India, the Muslims had necessarily to depend upon the inland resource only. Naturally the Muslims were lagging behind in the field of education.

The Muslim philanthropic efforts and establishment of educational institutions in Tiruchirappalli and Thanjavur districts of the Cauvery delta region are highly appreciable. Now they cater to the needs of hundreds of students both Muslims and non-Muslims not only of that locality but also from all over Tamil Nadu; especially to say about Jamal Mohammed College of Tiruchirappalli and the Khadir Mohideen College of Adirampattinam in Thanjavur district. The latter institution established by M.K.N. Madrasa trust, is located in an offshore coastal area serving the cause of education to the local and rural population. But for this college the education would have been denied to many and they would not have become graduates and postgraduates in this region. Even though the college was established for the benefit of minority Muslim community, in reality it is serving to the need of the all others too. Infact out of the total strength of 2,000 students studying in Khadir Mohideen College in the academic year 2004-05 only 400 students were Muslims.

The educational service (both modern and religious) of the Marraikkayars of Adirampattinam to the people of this remote off shore region is a thankless job. Even though there were many rich people in other communities only the Marraikkayars pioneered the cause of the education. The Muslim population of Tamil Nadu is not even one-tenth to its total population, yet they have made considerable contribution to the growth of education of the State. But in quite contradiction to this fact the Muslims are still lagging behind in the advancement of education.

The spread of Modern education in Tiruchirappalli and Thanjavur districts had brought in its train socio-economic changes. The result of the comparative analysis of the conditions present some fifty years ago with that of the conditions prevailing now shows that the Muslims women of these regions have progressed in their education to some extent. However, they have still a long way to go to achieve their empowerment. It is also true that their conditions are improving day-by-day and far better than their position some twenty years back. The general life style and status of the Muslims have improved and their industries and business received a modernization as a result of their educational development. An overall assessment of the social, economic and political conditions of the Muslims of these regions definitely showed an improving trend because of their educational empowerment and there is a wide scope to progress further in the future also. The impact of Modern education has been very much realized by the Muslims of Tiruchirappalli and Thanjavur districts, their educational institutions bear a witness to it.

In the survey done as a part of this thesis and from the personal experience, it is found that the Muslims of Thanjavur district are more literate than their counterparts in other districts. This is mainly due to the contact and affinity with the Brahmin community of this district in their day-to-day life especially in their trade activities. They happened to learn more, which elevated them to a higher place in literacy than the Muslims of other districts. This ultimately resulted in making the district to stand first in literacy during the Madras Presidency period and even now in Tamil Nadu.

The advantages of the modern education are understood by the Muslim community. The Muslim intellectualism changed its pattern from medievalism to modernism; this does not mean that Muslim intellectualism is useless, but not up to date. The Indian literature, both Hindu and Muslim, of Pre-British India did not include any work on nationalism. One of the causes for the rise of Indian nationalism, especially among the Muslims was the enlightenment attained through the English education. Syed Murthuza, Khaja Mian Rawther and

Jamal Mohammed of Tiruchirappalli and Abdul Hammeed (I.N.A) and Ibrahim Maraikkar (martyr) of Adirampattinam deserve a special mention here.The Muslim society felt the need to change its policy, attitude and superstitious beliefs about the Modern education because of the efforts taken by the intellectuals of their community. The Muslims feared in the beginning that the learning of Western education will bring an opportunity to the Muslim youth to inculcate the European manners and habits. But this hypothesis formed in general was not correct. For example, both Muhammad Ali Jinnah and Abul Kalam Azad were well-learned men; Jinnah developed western manners and customs whereas Abul Kalam Azad did not develop such things. So, inculcation of manners and habits purely depends upon the individual taste and not just by learning Western education.

The Muslim community came to know about the distortion of Indian history by the Britishers and other vested interested forces only after learning Modern education. The study of the English language thus provided an opportunity to the Muslims to study the social libertarian, natural scientific and rationalist philosophical literature in that language. Because of the Western learning the educated Muslims came to know the English democratic principles like 'all are equal before law' and the reversal of the same by the Britishers in India, which induced more Muslims to take active participation in the freedom movement. The Muslims advanced their intellectualism by learning the knowledge of modern scientific world through their study of English education and the same was transmitted to their own people.

The introduction of the Modern education and the acceptance of the same by the Muslims opened a new era in the educational advancement of the Muslims. As a result of this, Muslims attained progress in economic, political and social fields. Further, English learned Muslim middle class and intelligentsia rose in the Muslim community. The acceptance of Western education by the Muslims proved that the Muslims were not indifferent to knowledge or wisdom, but they were indifferent to British and their cultural traits only.

Despite the development in the education of the Muslims, the educated middle class in the community is very less. An overwhelming population of the Muslim community still remains illiterate. The percentage of educated women-folk in Muslim community is very meagre. The main reasons for this state of condition are their poverty and oppression of the women by men. The affluent group of the Muslim society is not ready to devote their resources for the welfare of the community. The step to eliminate mass poverty prevailing among the Muslims is not yet begun. Particularly in Tamil Nadu, a comprehensive plan of socio-economic reconstruction is not tried by the Muslims. A free and economically prosperous Muslim society alone could evolve a promotion of education and social services. It is not yet developed up to the requirement of Muslim community.

The conditions of the educational institutions of the Muslims are not up to the mark. Those who have started educational institutions, excepting a very few, in due course of time became educational entrepreneurs. The real visionary and passionate philanthropic attitudes in the affluent group of Muslim community have not come up with full bloom. Therefore the liquidation of mass illiteracy still remains as a problem before them.

There is a discontentment prevailing among the Muslims that the Central and the State Governments are not giving importance to the educational and economical development of the Muslims as it is given to the majority community. They demand for the right implementation of the Fundamental Rights guaranteed to the Muslim minority under Articles 26 to 30 of the constitution. In the course of the survey the researcher met some Muslims who opined that the Muslims should become a self-sufficient and self-dependant community without always having to rely on the Governments, which call themselves secular. And the Muslims should emulate the example of the Parsi, the Sikh and the Christian communities in making themselves non-dependant on the Government in the field of education. They also said that there was still enough wealth available with the affluent members of the Muslim community, provided that they cease to be niggardly for the cause of education and if properly materialized will take the community towards the empowerment and positive progress for the betterment of the community.

In the technical and technological field also, the picture is gloomy, none better so for as the Muslim minority community is concerned there is still great need every year to bring home to the Government the just needs of the minority Muslim community in the matter of admissions to the medical, engineering and other professional colleges. The community does not secure its due share even on population ratio. The Muslims should demand it as their legitimate right and press upon the Government.

The Muslim educational institutions established by the philanthropic munificence of the Muslim community also cater very largely to the needs of the majority community. Restrictions imposed in the matter of the medium of instruction, the matter of admissions, with regard to reservation of seats for the minority community, by whom these institutions are established and above all in the matter of inclusion of religious instruction in the regular curriculum are to be liberalized by the State Government. The Universities are playing an important role in the promotion of higher education; if they liberalize the conditions on minority institutions there is a scope for improvement and expansion of the educational activities of the minority communities.

As a self proclaimed secular state, India shows equal respect to all religions and maintains equal distance from all religions. But there has been violation of this principle in the recent years; it changes from one Government to another. Moreover there is an ambiguity in the case of India's domestic policy and affirmative action to uplift the Muslim community.

According to India's constitutional setup Hinduism as understood includes the Sikhs, the Buddhists and the Jains. Schedule castes and schedule tribes also come under the fold of Hinduism. But Muslims want to keep their religious identity and remain as a separate group. Most of the Muslims in India are converts from various sects in India especially from the downtrodden people. So, as a social justice, the reservation quotas and concessions extended to other sects may also be extended to the Muslim community as well.

The problem of religious education has assumed an uncompromising proportion towards secular education. This apparent conflict has to be solved, for Muslims there are no watertight compartments for religious and secular education, as such. These two aspects of education require to become integrated into one healthy whole, so that the system of education that is imparted in several theological colleges, Madrasas and seminaries becomes useful for the students in their every day life, not merely to lead a pious life but also to enable them to eke out their livelihood in an honourable manner. Mere employment as Moazzins and Pesh-Imams in mosques or as religious instructors in Maktabs and schools will never solve the economic problem of a Muslim in the present context of the world. It is also an object of an educational system to prepare students for practical life.

The world has become competitive in every walk of life and that the Muslims could not survive if they do not rise to the occasion. They should face the challenges with all efficiency and such efficiency can be attained only through their education. There should be an "All-India Muslim Educational Association" to look after all the educational economic and cultural interests of the Muslim community in India as a whole. Association of this kind need not concern itself with politics; instead it should have members from all parties, so that when a problem arises it can deal it with political standpoint. There was already an organization existing in the name of "All-India Educational Conference", but after independence it became lifeless and the organization lost its direction and pace. It has become inactive and it has ceased to serve many useful purposes for various reasons. It should be rejuvenated and brought to full-fledged action.

The most important matter to be considered by the Muslim community with zeal and earnestness is women's education especially their higher education. Ninety nine percent of the Muslim girls are not given the chance of pursuing their higher education; this is a very deplorable condition of the Muslim community. In the perspective of prejudice towards female education, it is surmised that almost the whole country has long been the victim of narrow mindedness, and aversion to female education. But the Muslims have been more ruthless and conservative. A good reason for illiteracy and backwardness of Muslims has been that they had no penchant for female education, but this has changed now. Now-a-days the Muslim girls are coming forward to take up the advantages of the higher education. Early marriages, non-availability of suitable bride groom (if the girl has higher educational qualification) and appalling poverty are some of the greatest stumbling blocks in the path of the education of women. It should be removed with all efforts of the community.

Some years ago, the attitude of Muslims towards female education was very bad which could be gauged by an instance of event that occurred in a liberal institution such as Mohammedan Anglo Oriental College where Sheikh Abdullah (an exponent of the Muslim female education) put forth a proposal to establish a school for the girls. His proposal was vehemently opposed by the conservative Muslims. By the organized efforts of Sheikh Abdullah a girls' school was established in 1907, which is today a unique residential institution for the female education in the all India level. Nearly 4,000 girls from various parts of the country from the primary to the higher level are receiving their education from that institution. Like this, in Tamil Nadu Justice Basheer Ahmed Syed was the pioneer of the promotion of Muslim girls' education. He founded SIET College for women in Madras (this is now called as Justice Basheer Ahmed Syed College for Women) in 1951 unmindful of the criticism commented on this effort. He could be called as 'Sir Syed Ahmed Khan of South India.' In the last few years, the Muslims had realized the significance of women's education and are paying their attention to it. Some of the Muslim Organizations have stressed their demand for the creation of a Muslim Women's University and the Anjuman-i-Islam in particular even prepared the plan for setting up a Muslim Women University in Maharastra or in Chennai. The progress of the community concerned is not merely with the male population alone, but largely by the liberal education of the women also, and it has to be realized by the Muslim community

The Muslim community of Tamil Nadu has a unique characteristic feature in the field of education, for example, even though the it has only 35 lakhs of Muslim population, it has 22 Arts and Science colleges to its credit whereas Uttara Pradesh which has more than three crores of Muslim population has only 29 Arts and Science colleges to its credit. This shows the enthusiasm and the zeal of the Muslims of Tamil Nadu in the promotion of education to their community.

In the recent years, the curriculum in Hindi belt states was given a communal colour; because of this trend the Muslim children keep aloof from the Government schools whereas in Tamil Nadu there is no such attempt. There is a scope for bright and better future for the education of the Muslims, provided they come forward and devote their energy and resources for the cause of education. Whenever there is a provocation and inimical acts of the opponents to the Government measures and reforms for the welfare of the minority community, the Government should take a firm stand and implement them without any hesitation.

The main difference between the Muslims of North and the Muslims of South especially of Tamil Nadu is the Northern Muslims emphases much on traditional and religious system of education whereas the Southern Muslims are afford to meet the demands of the modern age and opt more for the Western educational system. But this does not mean that they have no liking for religious education, instead they understand the need of the hour. Generally the educational dropout among the Muslim children is more than other communities and the cause for this state of affair is their poor economic condition. To eliminate this drop out condition attention must be paid by the affluent people of the community to provide them technical and professional courses to earn their livelihood and emancipate themselves from poverty. According to a survey report, in Tamil Nadu, if 100 Muslim children are admitted in the first standard, the number decreases to 30 when they reach the fifth standard. So, measures must be taken to bring back the 70 per cent dropout into the fold of education.

The Muslim community has to impress upon the Government with homogenous effort to assert and enforce its fundamental rights on education as dignified citizens with the sense of honour and self-respect. The Muslim community should also take up the full responsibility for the education of its youth, both men and women, from the beginning to the end, without purely depending upon Government assistance or grants. The Muslim community should traverse and explore the resources of the community and shall find the funds in ample measure. The community must so organize as to be self-reliant and self-dependant and survive the struggle for existence in this competitive world. This could be achieved only through a liberal education in Arts, Sciences and Technical fields, to the boys and girls of the community.

Moreover, the Muslims have to concentrate more on imparting knowledge to their youth in the field of information technology also. The Muslims do not have proper information about the Muslims Managed Educational Institutions spread all over the country. They are under the general impression that the community is far aloof from advanced education. Hence, an information centre like 'Guidance Cell' should be established so as to supply proper information and counseling to the Muslim students. The Muslim community must show itself that it has come to the conclusion that Muslims have included education into their agenda and despite their limited resources. If the Muslim intellectuals happen to come in a big way and enthusiastically for the guidance of institutions established for the welfare of the community, it would certainly gear up the educational, social and economical future of the Muslims of Tamil Nadu.

Glossary

Aalim	-	Religious scholar, expert
Fatwa	-	Religious judgement
Hadish (Hadith)	-	Traditions of the Prophet
Hafiz Quran	-	One who byhearted Quran
Hanafi	-	One of the four schools of thought in Islam
Halqahs	-	Group sitting, circle, locality
Ilm	-	Knowledge.
Kitabat	-	Writing meant for elementary religious education
Maktab	-	Muslim elementary school
Moulvi	-	Religious learner person
Muallim	-	Teacher in a Maktab
Mullah	-	Religious scholar
Munsiff	-	Just man
Mushi	-	Urdu Teacher
Niswan	-	Religious school for women
Niyyat	-	Intention or Aim
Pyall schools	-	Hindu temple schools
Qazi	-	Judge
Sabbath	-	Saturday
Sathaqua	-	Charity
Shafi	-	One of the four schools of thought in Islam
Shariah	-	Islamic law
Sunnah	-	Prophet's way of life
Ulemma	-	Religious heads
Wakf	-	Religious endowment
Zakath	-	Religious Charity

Bibliography

PRIMARY SOURCES

Arhival Sources

(A) Annual Reports

Annual Reports of the *Anjuman-i-Himayath-i-Islam,* Tamil Nadu Archives.

Annual Reports of the *Anjuman-i-Mufid-i-Ahle-i-Islam,* T N A.

Annual Reports of the *Hobart Higher Secondary and Training School for Muslim Girls,* Madras, T N A.

(B) Census Reports

Census of Madras Town, Report on the Result of the Educational Census of Madras, 1871, T N A.

Report on the Census of the Madras Presidency, 1881, T N A.

Report on the Census of the Madras Presidency, 1891, T N A.

Report on the Census of the Madras Presidency, 1901, T N A.

Report on the Census of the Madras Presidency, 1911, T N A.

Report on the Census of the Madras Presidency, 1921, T N A.

Report on the Census of the Madras Presidency, 1931, T N A.

First Report on Religion, Census of India, 2001, T N A.

(C) Government Orders (1882-1967)

Government Orders from Law and Education Department, T N A.

Government Orders from Education Department, T N A.

Government Orders from Law and Public Health Department, T N A.

Government Orders from Home and Education Department, T N A.

(D) Government Publications

Arbuthnot, A.J., *The Education of the Muhammadan Community in 1871,* New Delhi, 1964, T N A.

Baliga, B.S., *Selection from the Educational Records of the Government, 1859-71.*, New Delhi, 1960, National Archives.

Boag, G.T., *The Madras Presidency – 1881-1931*, Madras, 1957, T N A.

(E) Proceedings

Proceedings of Education Department, (1882-1967) , T N A.

Proceeding of Home Department, (1885-1924), T N A.

Proceeding of Home and Public Department, (1885-1924), T N A.

Proceeding of Local and Municipal Department, (1882-1967), T N A.

Proceedings of Revenue Department, (1882-1967), T N A.

(F) Quinquennial Reports, Educational

1886–87 to 1892–93, Volume I, Madras, 1893, T N A.

1902–03 to 1906–07, Volume I, Madras, 1907, T N A.

1906–07 to 1911–12, Volume I, Madras, 1912, T N A.

1916–17 to 1921–22, Volume I, Madras, 1922, T N A.

1926–27 to 1931–32, Volume I, Madras, 1932, T N A.

(G) Reports

Educational Survey Report, on Muslim Managed Schools and Colleges in India, Hamdard Education Society, New Delhi,1982-83, N A.

Interim Report on Education, Calcutta, 1929, T N A.

Memorandum on the Progress of Education in British India, 1916-1926, T N A.

Memoranda of the Government in India and the Indian Statutory Commission,1930, T N A.

Memoranda of the Madras Government on the Working of the Reformed Government, (Madras, 1930), T N A.

Progress of Education in India, 1902–1947, T N A.

Progress of Education in British India, 1922–1927, T N A.

Post War Educational Developments Reports in India by Central Advisory Board of Education Delhi, 1844, T N A.

Reports on the Administration of Madras Presidency, 1880 – 1947 A.D, T N A.

Reports on the Education Commission, Part 1, 1881–1882, T N A.

Reports on the Education Commission, Part 2, 1883, T N A.

Review of Education in India in 1886 with special reference to the reports of the Education Commission 1882, T N A.

Reports on the Public Instruction in the Madras Presidency, 1880 – 1947A.D, T N A.

Report on the Mohammedan Educational Endowment Committee, printed at the Bengal Secretariat Press, Calcutta, 1888, National Archives.

Report of the Madras Provincial Committee Memorials addressed to the Education Commission, T N A.

Report on the Elementary of Madras Presidency, 1924–1925 (Madras, 1925), TNA.

Report of the Private Institutions in the Madras Presidency (Madras, 1898), T N A.

Report of the Indian Universities Commission, 1902, T N A.

Resolution of Educational Policy, 1904, T N A.

Resolution of Educational Policy, 1913, T N A.

Review of the Progress of Education in India, 1947-52, Delhi, 1953, T N A.

The Annual Reviews of Education in India from 1913–1939, T N A.

In India, (1982-83) Hamdard Education Society, New Delhi, N A..*Report of the Mohammedans Educational Endowments Committee,* printed by Secretariat Press, Calcutta, 1888, N A.

SECONDARY SOURCES

(A) Articles

Abdul Rahman,B.S., and Sathika, 'Development and Alternatives for Educationof Islamic Youth and Role of United Fconomic Forum', *Al-Ameen Monthly Organ, Al-Ameen Educational Society,* Bangalore, 1983.

Ahmad Karuna, From Secondary to Higher Education, Focus on Women, *'Journals of Higher Education'* Volume-IX, New Delhi, 1984.

McPherson, K., 'The Social Background and Politics of the Muslims of Tamilnadu. 1907-1937, *IESHR,* Vol.VI, 4th December, 1969, pp. 381-402.

Mines, Mattison, 'Islamisation and Muslim Ethnicity in South India', *Man, Journals of Royal Anthropological Institute* Vol. 10, No. 3, New Delhi, 1975.

More, J.B.P., "The Marakkayar Muslims of Karikal. South India", *Journal of Islamic Studies,* Vol. II, No. 1, 1991, pp. 25-44.

Muhammed, Peer, 'The Problem of the Eductional Backwardness of Indian Muslims' *Guru Nanak Journal of Sociology,* Amritsar,1984.

Rahim, Abdul M., 'Islam in Nagapatnam', *Bulletin of the Institute of Traditional Cultures,* Madras, July-December, 1974, pp. 85-99.

Robinson, F., 'Islam and Muslim Society in South Asia', *Contributions to Indian Sociology,* Vol. VII, No. 2, 1983.

Robinson, F., 'Islam and Muslim Separatism', Political Identity in South Asia, *David Taylor and Malcolm Yapp (eds)*, London, 1979, pp. 78-112.

Syed, S., 'Urdu Journalism in Tamil Nadu from 1940 to 1950', Annals of Oriental Research, Vol-XXVII, Part-I and Part-II.

(B) Books

Abrar, Rahat, *OMEIAT Directory of Muslim Educational institutions in Tamil Nadu*, Aligarh Publications, Aligarh 2000.

Ahmad, Aziz, *Studies in Islamic Culture in the Indian Environment*, Oxford University Press, London, 1964.

Ahmad, Imtiaz (ed.), *Caste and Social Stratification among the Muslims*, Delhi, 1973.

Ahmad, Imtiaz, *Educational Development of Minorities*, APH Publication Corporation, New Delhi, 1989.

Basu, B.D., *History of Education in India, under the Rules of East India Company*, Calcutta, 1971.

Bhatnagar, S.K., *History of the M.A.O College Aligarh*, Aligarh Publications, Aligarh, 1969.

Boag, G.T., *The Madras Presidency 1881-1931*, Government Press, Madras, 1933.

Chitnis, K.N., *Socio-economic History of Mediaeval India*, Atlantic Publishers, New Delhi, 1976.

Desai, A.R., *Social Background of Indian Nationalism*, Popular Prakashan Publications, Bombay, 1986.

Edgar, Thurston, *Castes and Tribes of South India*, Vol. IV, 1909.

Farquhar, J.N., *Modern Religious Movements in India*, First Indian edition, Delhi, 1967.

Frykenberg, R.E., *Modern Educaction in South India 1784 to 1854*, American History Review, Vol.91, No.1, 1986, pp. 37-65.

Ghosh, Suresh Chandra, *Education Policy in India Since Warren Hastings*, Naya Prakash, Calcutta, 1979.

Gopal, R., *Indian Muslims: A Political History 1858 - 1947*, Bombay, 1959.

Hampton, H.V., *Biographical Studies in Modern Indian Education*, Oxford University Press, New Delhi, 1947.

Hardy, Peter, *The Muslims of British India*, Cambridge, 1972.

Hunter, W.W, *The Indian Musalmans*, reprinted from the 3rd edition, London (1876), New Delhi, 1969.

Jaffar S.M., *Education in Muslim India*, Reprint, Delhi, 1972.

Kaur, Kuldip, *Madrasa Education in India, Its Past and Present,* Published by Center for Research and Industrial Development, Chandigarh, 1990.

Kunhan Raja, C., *Progress of Education in Tamil Nadu,* New Era Publications, Madras, 1978.

Mcpherson, K.,*The Political Development of Urdu and Tamil Speaking Muslims of the Madras Presidency,1901-1937,* unpublished M.A., Dissertation, University of Western Australia, 1968.

Mines, Mattison, *Social Stratification among Muslim Tamils in Tamilnadu,* in Caste and Social Stratification among Muslims in India, Imtiaz Ahamad (ed.), Delhi, 1978, pp.61-71.

More J.B.P., *The Political Evolution of Muslims in Tamil Nadu and Madras, 1930-1947,* Orient Longman Ltd, 1997.

Murex, M., *The Indian Muslims,* London, 1967.

Nurullah, S. and Naik, J.P., *A History of Education in India,* Popular Prakashan, Bombay, 1951

Picktall, Marmaduke, *Quran-i-Majid, Al-asant,* Rampur, 1980.

Rahim, Abdul, M.R.M., *Islamiya Kalai Kalanjiyam,* Hindustan Publications, Madras, 1976.

Rasheed, A.A., *A Brief History of the MEASI and the New College,* Madras, 1971.

Rifaye, A.K., *Tamizhakathil Islamiyar Varalaaru,* Nushrat Publications, Tenkasi, 1988.

Robinson, Francis, *Separatism among Indian Muslims, the Politics of United Provinces Muslims, 1860-1923,* Oxford University Press, London, 1994.

S. Ghosh, Partha, Director, '*Affirmative Action in India*', Indian Council of Social Science Research, New Delhi, 1998, N A.

Saxena, Abha, *Indian National Movement and the Liberals,*Chugh Publications, Allahabad, 1986.

Sayeed, Basheer Ahamad, *My Life, A Struggle: An Autobiography,* Madras, 1983.

Smith, W.C., *Modern Islam in India,* London, 1946.

Sulaiman, S.M., M.M. Ismail, *Islam, Indian Religions and Tamil Culture,* Madras, 1977.

Suresh Chandra Ghose, *EducationPolicy in India since Warren Hastings,*Naya Prakash Publications,Calcutta,1971.

Syed, Muhammad, *A Concise but Correct History of the Muslim Educational Association of Southern India and New College,* Madras, 1977.

Vaikuntham, Y., *Education and Social Changes in the Madras Presidency: Andhra, 1880 – 1920 A.D,* New Era Publications, Madras, 1986.

(C) Encyclopaedia

Encyclopaedia Britannica, Volume-XII, London, 1966.

Encyclopaedia of Ethics and Religion (ed) by James Hastings, Volume-VIII, Edinburgh, 1967.

Encyclopaedia of Islam, Volume-I, London, 1960.

The World Book Encyclopaedia, Volume-IX, Chicago, 1960.

(D) Gazetteers and Manuals

Imperial Gazetteer of India

Madras District Gazetteers

Madras District Manuals

Manual of the Administration of the Madras Presidency, Volume I.

Manual of the Administration of the Madras Presidency, Volume II.

Tanjore District Hand Book, B.S. Baliga, Curator, Madras Record Office, Egmore, 1957.

District Census Hand Book, Tiruchirappalli, 1901-70.

A Manual of the Trichinopoly District in the Presidency of Madras, Lewis Moore, M.C.S, 1878.

Madras District Gazetteers, Trichinopoly District, F.R. Hemingway, 1907.

(E) Newspapers and Magazines

Native Newspaper Reports from 1879–1946.

Asylum Press Almanac from 1894–1919.

The Indian Ladies Magazine from 1903–1937.

Stri Dharma from 1920–1939.

The Madras Year Book, 1923.

The Madras Year Book, 1931.

Madras Information, 1946 and 1947.

(F) Souvenirs

History of Higher Education in Southern India, Centenary Commemoration of the University of Madras 1857-1957, Vol.I and II, Associate Printers, Madras, 1957.

Government Hobart Higher Secondary and Training School for Muslim Women, Madras 1873–1973, Centenary Souvenir, Souvenir Committee, Madras, 1973.

*Hobart Higher Secondary and Training School for Muslim Women, Madras 1873–1999,*Post Silver Jubilee Centenary Souvenir, Madras, 1999.

The Anjuman-i-Mufid-i-Ahle Islam, Centenary Celebration Souvenir,

Madras, 1885-1995.

*The Muslim Educational Association of Southern India, Madras,*Diamond Jubilee Souvenir, 1902-1962, Madras, 1964.

The Anjuman-i-Himayath-i-Islam, Souvenir 2000, Madras, 2000.

The New College Staff Golden Jubilee Celebrations, (2001-02), Golden Leaf Souvenir Committee, Madras, 2001-2002.

Founder Principal Alhaj M.J. Mohamed Sayeed Saheb, Birth Centenary Celebrations Souvenir, Jamal Mohammed College, Tiruchirappalli 2003.

Founder's day, Special issue Souvenir, Jamal Mohammed College, Golden Jubilee Celebrations, Tiruchirappalli, 2000–2001.

Khadir Mohideen College Golden Jubilee Celebrations Souvenir, Editorial Committee, Khadir Mohideen College, Adirampattinam, 2005.

Abdullah College for Women Magazine, Aligarh Muslim University Campus, Aligarh, 1901–02.

(G) Unpublished Ph.D. Thesis

Peer Mohammad., *History of Progress of Education in Madras City, 1854-1947,* University of Madras, 1998.

Hassan, R.B.M.R., *The Educational Movement of Sir Syed Khan, 1858-1898,* London,1960.

Hassina Begum, *Education of Muslim Women in the Presidency of Madras (with a special reference to the city of Madras) - 1854-1947,* University of Madras, 2001.

Sarguru Dos, *History of Education in Madras Presidency, 1800-1900,* University of Madras, 1969.

Sathiyanathan, *History of Education in the Madras Presidency,* University of Madras, 1971.

(H) Other Sources

Annual Reports of the *Haja Mian Higher Secondary School,* Tiruchirappalli, 1999-2000.

Annual Reports of the *Islamiah College,* Vaniyambadi, 1998-99.

Annual Reports of the *Justice Basheer Ahmed Syed College for Women,* 2001-02.

Annual Reports of the *Jamal Mohammad College,* Tiruchirappalli, 2000-01.

Annual Reports of the *Khadir Mohideen College,* Adirampattinam, 2001-02.

Annual Reports of the *Muslim Girls' School,* George Town, Chennai, 2000-01

The 101st Annual Reports of the *Muslim Educational Association of Southern India,* 2003.

Annual Reports of the New College, Chennai, 2000-01. Fort St. George Gazette, Madras.

Index

N

O

P

Q

R

S

T

U

V

W

Z